Japan
Reports from an Enigmatic Land

Gert Anhalt

Contents

1 Festive kimonos for "Coming-of-Age Day". **2** Typical front yard in bonsai size. **3** One of the very last samurai. **4** Plum blossoms – harbingers of spring. **5** A couple of goldfish in plastic bags in front of someone's door. **6** Cool, but conscious of traditions. **7** Famous "Spectacles Bridge" (megane-bashi) in Nagasaki. **8** True love. **9** Sushi, Japan's favorite dish. **10** Nap on Dad's cool box. **11** Traditional house front. **12** Cook shop for cabbage pancakes.

Japan is overwhelming. It is confusing and mysterious. It is challenging. It raises our curiosity, stimulates our imagination and requires our patience.

Whoever takes time for Japan and discovers it, whoever travels through the country and gets to know it, will either love or hate it, will either admire it or smile at it.

Japan will astonish its visitors, will amuse them, inspire them and maybe it will cast its spell on them. But one thing is for sure: nobody will remain indifferent to this country… Incredibly large crowds of people are quite common in Japan. People come together in huge numbers where there is something to marvel at, such as a fireworks display or a *matsuri*. In the city of Suwa, the *Onbashiri-Matsuri* is a worthwhile reason to get together.

Yokoso – Welcome to Japan!

…this is how the new colorful posters of the Japanese Tourism Association welcome us upon our arrival at Tokyo airport. It is part of an international campaign – Japan wants to finally establish itself as a tourism destination. This hasn't been too successful so far. Most visitors to Japan are business people – stressed sales strategists, smart managers, engineers and experts with little time for a proper, calm look at this amazing island nation. Japan is not a particularly attractive destination for tourists. It is too expensive, too complicated, too far away.

On top of that, our knowledge of this country, beyond that of the tight circle of Japanologists and serious Japanophiles, is blurred by prejudices, half truths and clichés. More than once I felt deeply embarrassed when I noticed how much the educated Japanese know about our history and culture, while for most of us Japan really still is an unknown country, an enigmatic land.

And this is despite the fact that you can pick up sushi at almost every street corner now and manga heroes dominate the imagination of our kids. And it doesn't matter that Japanese design stimulates the creativity of our architects and interior decorators and that Japanese cars and electronics have long become part of our everyday life. The country where all these familiar things come from remains strange to us and – in the worst case – even a little scary. In any case, somehow weird.

Admittedly Japan is quite a challenge. It took me five years to learn the language and I am still lost for words far too often and stumble over characters which I've never seen before or which I've simply forgotten. Its society has completely different rules and laws from ours, and as foreigners we will probably never feel com-

pletely comfortable in it. This country intimidates us with its densely populated landscapes, its mountain slopes covered in concrete, its spoilt coastlines, its hopelessly built-up cities, its typhoons, volcanoes, earthquakes, long queues, complicated toilets and overcrowded subways.

But on the other hand Japan takes our breath away with its incredible beauty, its pristine nature, its heartwarming friendliness, its excessive cheerfulness, its indescribable culinary delights, and the refreshing realization that everything works just as well in a completely different way from what we are used to and what we think is right.

I have spent many years here and still not a day passes where I don't come across something new, unsuspected, something that astounds me, delights me or occasionally also annoys me. For me, Japan is the biggest bag of surprises in the world. A parallel universe which is sometimes better than ours, often more interesting and always astonishing, and which works according to its own set of rules, pretty resistant to globalization efforts. One side firmly embedded in history and tradition and the other in the distant future. Traveling in this country will be rewarded with unforgettable impressions and experiences. Living in this country for a while is a privilege.

I will try to surprise you a little. I will tell you a few things about Japan which you may not know. And I will show you pictures which you may never have seen, or at least not very often.
So please don't be disappointed if I don't present karate fighters, capsule hotels, calligraphers and bonsais and only a few geishas. And please don't be disappointed if my sumo wrestlers don't wrestle, but make babies cry instead.

After all it is supposed to be a trip to an enigmatic land…

1 A cup of green tea is part of every welcome and every meeting.
2 Snow country – in winter Nigata is buried under a thick snow blanket, 3–4 meters deep. 3 Carp and cherry blossoms symbolize Japan's sense of aesthetics. 4 The dramatic coast of the Izu Peninsula, only two hours drive from Tokyo.

No Trepidation About of Unknown Worlds

It is quite normal that we can't help feeling a little shy when we begin exploring an unknown country. Yet there is absolutely no need to panic, even though it sometimes helps to plug one's ears.

Open Your Eyes Wide, Block Your Ears – and Go!

A quick tour through Tokyo

We should start our journey with something you can't see, contemplate or read. Let us begin with the sounds of Japan. It is the morning of a mild spring day and while I am writing this in a part of Tokyo's inner city that is not known to be particularly manic, I can hear a pneumatic hammer out there, eating its way through the tarmac, for they are once again ripping open the street in the neighborhood. Incidentally construction work continues night and day here, in fact preferably at night to avoid any additional disruption to the traffic, which is often comatose as it is. A crane is grumbling, too, as a new high-rise building is going up at the main street. Occasionally I can hear a siren howling in the distance, accompanied by the ambulance driver's announcements. "I will be crossing the red light now, please be careful!" If the wind were blowing from the right direction, I'd also be able to hear the jingling of a grade crossing and the rhythmic rattle of the trains hurrying by every minute. A raven has settled on the tree in front of my window. It is an ugly black animal that utters horrible croaking noises, which his crow friend on the opposite roof responds to with similar horrible croaking noises. Today they are running quite late. Usually their conference, to which they like to invite other raven colleagues as well, commences at 6 o'clock in the morning. It is almost summer. That's when the *semi* arrive, the notorious cicadas with the jet fighter motors that only miss their usual cue at sunrise around 4.30 am when it is pouring heavily. The electro-garbage collector just drove by. (Which is due only because I really want to mention him, for he usually starts his rounds on Sunday mornings at 8.30. Today it's Saturday). As always he drives along at a snail's pace. He has a loudspeaker mounted on his roof through which he slowly lists all the broken electric appliances that he tends to collect. He is quite loud, but friendly and his list is very long. When he's gone, there comes the guy who sells bamboo-washing poles, singing loudly *("Takeya-Saodakeeee…")*. On winter evenings he is joined by the sweet potato man who also sings at the top of his voice *("O-imo, o-imo, o-imo – ishiyaaki imo")*. If it were a patriotically significant date today, the black busses of the right wing radicals, equipped with war flags and loudspeakers would contribute to the acoustic background with blaring military marches, appeals for the

1 Special offers are usually accompanied by a lot of noise. **2** Tokyo's secret rulers – the cheeky ravens. **3** The most powerful weapon of the retail Samurai – his megaphone. **4** Awesome – Tokyo's sea of buildings. In wintertime, Mount Fuji is clearly visible.

adoration of the emperor and for the revolution and return of the Kuril Islands that are occupied by Russia. But today is just a normal Saturday. Somewhere someone is blowing a whistle to help a truck reverse. When the truck is about to take a left turn, a canned female voice announces: "I am about to take a left turn. Please be careful." This is accompanied by the ring of a bell.

In any event: Japan is home to ringing noises. And motherland to little, light tunes. The sounds of jingling, ringing or whistling are always erupting somewhere. Ringing noises are supposed to alert people to dangers and the little, cheerful tunes are designed to sweeten everyday life, to please people and maybe entice them to consume something or to attract their attention – at least temporarily. Ringing noises emanate from shop entrances, from dispensing machines and from the cell phones of people rushing by. Let's take a fun walk to Shibuya station, which isn't far, and wander through the shopping and entertainment area that has developed all around it. From almost every single one of the countless boutiques, shoe shops, karaoke towers and amusement arcades loudspeakers blares a different song. The noise level in the shops can easily reach 80 decibels or more – this is almost as loud as in a discotheque. Young men standing on boxes and ladders in front of the drugstores and shops for electric appliances use their strong voices (plus megaphones) to cry: *"Irasshaimasse, irasshaimasse!"*, welcoming the people rushing by and advertising their spectacular special offers. In the *pachinko* halls where the customers sit in long rows in front of blinking machines, similar to pin-ball machines, millions of small silver balls rattle with incredible force. If these pachinko halls were factories, its workers would undoubtedly have to wear ear protection. But the customers just sit there with a look of intense concentration, completely immune against the din. Yet all these different noises are a lullaby compared to the screeching of the brakes of a Japanese bike. Perhaps the noise is due to a lack of grease supply.

Or else it is due to the fact that the cyclists, who nonchalantly use the sidewalks, don't want to hurt the feelings of pedestrians by ringing their bells, so they brake instead. In any case, the local bicycle designers have apparently decided to supply the brakes with a penetrating, metallic primal scream, which gives you goose bumps. To some, it is the most horrid noise experience in our universe.

In front of the station sits another car equipped with loudspeakers and a man dressed in a suit is loudly arguing that American food such as hamburgers, French fries or fried chicken isn't good for the Japanese, as Japanese actually prefer to eat fish. The intended message is probably a more philosophical one – against globalization or the Americans or both. At any rate, transported by 500-watt loudspeakers, his voice booms over the crowd – which ignores it. One of the most astonishing abilities of the Japanese is their selective perception and their stoical patience when it comes to all kinds of sales people, idealists, politicians or scatterbrains with loudspeakers.

1 Girly picnic – black hair is truly out… **2** Careful! Pedestrians! Shopping area in the district of Shinjuku. **3** Boutiques, bars and restaurants in the lively backstreets of Shibuya. **4** Here the fronts of the buildings look as though manga artists have designed them.

Announcements at the station. Announcements in the train. The train is about to arrive. Please stand back behind the yellow line! This is Shibuya station. Please don't push! Please don't leave anything behind in the carriage! Switch your cell phone to vibration mode to avoid disturbing the other passengers! Thank you for choosing this line. Take care, the doors are closing now! The exit is not longer on the left hand side; it is now on the right hand side. All these announcements are interspersed and interrupted by nerve wracking ringing tones several times.

Beyond any doubt, Japan is the worldwide leader in considerate loudspeaker announcements. As if the authorities feared that they are dealing with a nation of clumsy people who are in constant danger of marching off in the wrong direction towards a disaster, of getting lost, of choking on something or of falling into construction pits. Keep going, walk slowly, move quickly! Keep to the right! This way! Careful, you've reached the end of the escalator! Watch your feet! It can really be annoying, but still: one becomes accustomed to them. Even worse, you get used to them to such an extent that you start feeling positively insecure when there are none. Am I behaving correctly? This anxious question is the Leitmotif of Japanese daily life anyways.

So this nation doesn't stop ringing, jingling and issuing warnings. And with everything that is to be discovered in this country (with the exception of trips to the mountains or extensive forests and parks), you best always imagine some kind of background noise if you want to come as close as possible to the proper Japan feeling. Now I have suddenly led you to Shibuya. That's not quite fair, as this garish, loud part of town is not representative of Tokyo. It is always showcased in TV documentaries and movies, whenever the point is to be made that that Japan's capital city is a crazy fun fair, a kind of witches' cauldron bubbling over with nervously blinking ads and

gigantic monitors. A place where tanned blonde-dyed mini-skirted fashionistas and cool guys wearing sunglasses and toting strange hairstyles saunter along the labyrinthine course of the zebra crossings. This isn't Tokyo. But it is Shibuya. The train station and the area around it are so chaotic and bizarre, as though a manga artist had been asked to design it, without sparing loud colors. Shibuya is considered the Mecca for the modern youth and its shops and entertainment venues cater mainly to the tastes of minors. For the tastes of game boys and girlies plus their admirers and pursuers from the ranks of usually sexually disturbed public servants.

Tokyo is a kind of amorphous mass, a gigantic, but benign growth of a city. There is no perceivable city center, no downtown as defined in the West. Tokyo has several centers with clearly defined functions: shopping, entertainment, administration, government and traffic centers. Shibuya with its 600,000 inhabitants is just one of them. Another one is Shinjuku, three kilometers to the north, with its high-rise buildings, including offices and hotels. Up until recently

1 High-rise buildings in Shinjuku. This is Tokyo's version of a skyline. 2 Rush hour on the world-famous crossroads in front of Shibuya station. 3 The craze of silver balls – pachinko, Japan's pinball game. 4 Twelve million people live in Tokyo; over 30 million live in its surroundings. 5 Although Tokyo is regularly haunted by earthquakes, the city likes to rise high. 6 The elegant shopping street Ginza.

Shinjuku was the only place with anything resembling a skyline. Until just a few years ago, high-rise buildings were the exception in this city plagued by earthquakes. But now architects are trying to outdo each other with bold, sky-high constructions. At the turn of the millennium more than 60 high-rise buildings were under construction, in planning or had just been completed.

On top of that Tokyo has its fashion and window shopping centers, such as Ginza with its expensive department stores and the *Omote-sando* lined by numerous boutiques of famous European and national fashion designers and interior decorators. Nowadays you'll hardly find a young Japanese woman without a Louis-Vitton handbag. Least of all walking along the *Omote-sando.*

I must also mention Shinagawa, Ikeburo and Ueno, the main stations where the millions of commuters from the suburbs change trains. In the morning they are the sluices to their workplaces and in the evening they represent the gates to return back home. Incidentally, the many centers of Tokyo weren't invented suddenly.

They developed historically, as early as the medieval times, and represented the main traffic junctions to Edo, as Tokyo was known then.

But other than that Tokyo has retained sobering little history. One reason for this is that the city is regularly flattened by earthquakes – twice just in the last century. After the large earthquake of 1923 and the firebomb raids of the Americans in World War II, there wasn't much left of Tokyo. The other reason why there is almost no historical substance left is that the Japanese are not very romantic as far as caring for old buildings is concerned. At least not if they are expected to actually live in them. The old, dreamy houses that you still find in Tokyo – sometimes charmingly positioned right in between the smartest apartment and office buildings – usually belong to staunch old people who stubbornly refuse to move at their old age.

Admittedly Tokyo is, at least in parts, a single, huge attack on western ideas of town planning and on western sensibilities. A walk

Tokyo's trains – The most important mode of transport, apart from the cab, is the suburban train, which runs both above and underground. Its rails crisscross this enormous city like a spider web. **1 – 2** Regional trains and national trains thunder right past peoples' homes. **3** A train a minute – Tokyo's railway system is the most effective in the world. There are twelve lines covering a distance of 292 kilometers… **4** …and transport 7,5 million people every day… **5** …under and above ground plus a few stories high.

The Japanese and their signs

Not without a sense of admiration one will realize that it takes an exceptionally quick gift of perception to absorb all the information on the signs at Edobashi in northeastern Tokyo. The distances to the main centers Shinjuku, Shibuya and Ike-bukuro are indicated, next to the information that the toll for a car is 700 Yen and that for a truck is 1400 Yen (more than six and 13 Euros respectively). Incidentally, the toll is independent from the length of the trip. The illuminated sign right at

the top tells you that an accident has caused a traffic jam of many kilometers length right up to Kandabashi junction. Beneath that there's the warning that lethal motorcycles accidents increase at the weekend. In addition the many smaller signs provide information on the acceptable weight and dimensions of vehicles using this highway, the rule that trucks must keep on the right hand lane and that pedestrians have no business being on the highway. There is an express warning in red letters that speed limits should be adhered to in order to avoid accidents. Of course nobody complies with the speed limit of 80 km/h on Japan's highways. Many drive 100; most drive 120 km/h, some drive even faster.
In the tangle of signs the information gets lost. It is simply too much to take in. Presumably this problem is now being discussed by a commission of the Ministry of Transport, which will probably arrive at the conclusion that more signs are required urgently.

through certain parts, such as "electro town" Akihabara, which is plastered with garish billboards advertising special offers and home to computer games, monitors and cell phones, may seem like a walk through hell for those who are sensitive to noise and colors. But the terror of noise, flashing lights and billboards which you are usually exposed to near the train stations curiously only extends to the next corner, to the next crossroad. Then, completely unexpectedly and almost absurdly you'll come across a scene that you'd expect from a village. No Starbucks, McDonald's and big-echo karaoke. Far from it. A granny tends to her pot plants in front of her door, a housewife leans out of the open window to hang out her washing on the new bamboo poles which she just bought off the vendor of bamboo poles passing through her alleyway singing at the top of his voice. A delivery boy with his white cap hops onto his bike to deliver soba, noodles in a spicy broth. The charming, chaotic backstreets are narrow and congested, full of bikes, billboards, signs, the daily restaurant menus and grey power poles supporting the wildly tangled bunches and knots of telephone and

electricity cables all across town. Not dissimilar to the city high-way whose ramps and bridges sometimes wind their way through the concrete jungle two or three stories high, supported by massive pillars.

The best way to understand Tokyo is not to imagine it as a city, but as a humongous village blown up out of all proportion. Its smallest unit is the neighborhood that is, if everything takes its right course, overseen by an elder who is respected by all. Particularly in Tokyo's east, in shitamachi or "downtown", which represents the actual "old city" (although this term is misleading), the neighborhoods are intact, the streets are narrow, the atmosphere is calm and friendly and traditions are still alive.

If this city has any center, then it is the Emperor's Palace, a silent park-like property surrounded by grey stonewalls and broad moats. During the golden 80's of the past century, the years of the so-called bubble economy or soap bubble economy, its value was estimated as high as that of the entire US State of California in. The Emperor's Palace is not a sightseeing must, as it simply remains invisible and actually is nothing special in comparison with the real estate of other monarchs.

A few historical watchtowers, the bridges and the portals might be of some interest. The other option is walking around the palace for hours and visiting parts of the Emperor's Park.

The Emperor's presence in Tokyo has consequences for the entire country, including the railway traffic. All trains leaving Tokyo are *kudari,* descending, and consequently those heading for Tokyo are *nobori,* ascending. Japan also affords itself the luxury of its own calendar. Until today, the country calculates its time according to the tenure of the current emperor or Tenno and names it after a flowery reign motto. The current Emperor Akihito's motto is *heisei,*

1 The organized chaos of a construction site in Tokyo. Shift work ensures 24-hour noise for the neighborhood. **2** "Keep right, keep left, move on quickly!" The Japanese seem addicted to warnings issued via loudspeakers. **3** "Be careful!" Some of the narrow alleys are like obstacle courses. **4** Every rush hour: traffic jam on five levels – Tokyo's city highway.

The Birth of modern Japan

Since 794 the Japanese emperors and their court resided in Kyoto where they had nothing more exciting to do but to write pensive poems about the ways of the world and the beauty of autumn leafs. Meanwhile warriors and warlords and the military governors, the Shoguns, determined the destiny of the country. In 1868, after 267 years of military dictatorship and the complete isolation of the island empire, the Shogun system did not have the answers to some burning questions, such as: How does a railway system work? Or: What exactly happens in a factory. It became crystal clear that this country needed a jolt. This impetus was provided when the 122nd Tenno, according to mythical calculation, took the throne. It was the Meiji Tenno. To keep things simple, he is said to have been responsible for the entire modernization of Japan, although he was only fifteen years of age at the time. One of his first rulings was to move the government seat to Edo, where the Shoguns resided. Then he changed the name Edo to Tokyo and became head of state once more—which is why one talks about a restoration of the emperor's power. Modern Japan was born. It didn't take long before telephones, a parliament, electric blankets and French fries appeared. But before this happened the Meiji emperor died in 1912 and, as is customary, his kami, his spirit, and that of his wife were enshrined in the Meiji shrine.

Emperor behind bulletproof glass

Only twice a year, on New Year's Day and on the Emperor's birthday (currently December, 23), the public may access the property around the palace. On these days they can wave to the Tenno and his family with little Japan flags which are distributed at the entrance and which are collected again at the exit by boy scouts. The emperor and his family appear on a particular balcony and wave back – incidentally from behind bulletproof glass. Then the Emperor nasally mumbles a few non-committal words of thanks. Then he retreats, only to appear again to the next crowd of waving people waiting in front of the gates.

Japan's emperor has no political power. He is the "symbol of the nation and the unity of its people". He merely attends to a number of ceremonial matters and has representative duties at the behest of and in close coordination with the government. The Americans urgently wanted to take away the power

and magic of the Tenno who had been adored as a God so far. After all, Japan's soldiers had brought incredible suffering to an entire continent in his name. However, General MacArthur decided not to persecute the emperor personally for the war and its atrocities (even though at that time there were valid doubts as to his innocence), so as not to destabilize Japan. Isolated and controlled by the court's camarilla who are obsessed with tradition, the Tenno and his family now lead a positively unreal life, a life behind bullet-proof glass — very different to the somewhat vivacious monarchs of Europe.

One of the Tenno's duties is to give the festive speech on the Day of the Seas, the day when Japan's powerful fishery lobby celebrates itself. I once witnessed how the emperor and the empress ignored a murderous downpour with incredible courage and sense of humor and, soaked right through to the bone, took the salute at the parade of the fishing boats. In his speech the Tenno remembered having been brought to this area during the war: "At that time I watched the fish in an aquarium bump their noses against the glass again and again…" His words made me feel sad. It seemed as though he was referring to himself, his own imprisonment. But maybe I am wrong. What do I know about the thoughts of a lonely emperor?

which translates roughly as "origin of peace". Akihito's term commenced in 1989, thus the Japanese think of 2004 as *heisei 16*. His controversial father Hirohito ruled from 1926 to 1989, under the motto of *showa* "enlightened harmony". Therefore my driver's license tells me highly officially that I was born in the year of showa 38. Prior to Hirohito it was *taisho* (great virtue) Tenno's turn. Of ailing health and a little confused to some, he was emperor from 1912-1926. He took over from *meiji* (enlightened ruler) Tenno whose turbulent years of 1868-1912 marked the period of great changes and the era of the opening up of a country which had previously been shuttered from the world.

1 Lonely relic in the banking district – a watchtower near the Emperor's Palace. **2** Typical shopping street in the old city shitamachi. Not much has changed here… **3** An oasis of coziness and tradition: an old wooden house in the middle of the modern city center.

Take a Deep Breath!
Japan's overwhelming natural scenery

Enough now of lack of space, crowds and noise. Japan is not Tokyo. Just as little as the United States are synonymous with New York. Japan has an overwhelming natural environment. Its diversity is mesmerizing. But as we are usually fixated on Japan's high risers and zebra crossings which run diagonally over major junctions as well, we rarely become aware of it.

The truly unknown Japan starts only a couple of hour's drive away from the metropolis. In the valleys of the prefecture of Gunma, in the rice paddies and bamboo plantations of the prefecture of Chiba or along the ragged coast of the Izu peninsula. And if you dare venture even further from the capital city, you'll be quite amazed.

Let's have a look at Hokkaido, the northern island, for example. (By the way, please do not pronounce it as "Hokka-eedo" if you want to spare even the calmest Japanese studies expert a nervous breakdown. It will cause almost the same reaction as the awful "Fudjee-yama" which seems ineradicable.) Hokkaido is the Scandinavia and Alaska of Japan. It is comparatively thinly populated and its infrastructure is sparse. In winter it lies buried under snow drifts several meters high and it is more or less the only place in the entire country where there is sufficient room for happy cows to chew their cud on real pastures. Hokkaido is a place where the ubiquitous danger signs do not warn you about constructions sites and pits, but about real live bears which occasionally emerge from the dense forests to dine on unsuspecting hikers. It is the land of the lakes, forests and waterfalls, of the cranes and eagles, deer and foxes.

The north of the Japanese main island, Honshu, an area referred to as tohoku (north-eastern region), is similarly untamed. It is a region of canyons, roaring mountain streams and magnificent forest and mountain landscapes, such as the grandiose backdrop of Iwate-san, the volcano of 2,000 meters height. The ragged, rocky bays along the Pacific coast are dramatically beautiful as well. Yet to avoid disappointment, don't believe all the pictures you see, not even the ones in this book. Be prepared to come across a horrible auto graveyard or an ugly, bland harbor town right behind the most breathtakingly beautiful bay and the most magical of canyons. And don't

1 A couple of palm trees guard the southernmost tip of Kyushu, the beach at Mount Kaimon. 2 Bear cubs playing in Shiretoko National Park on Hokkaido. 3 Japan is the country of waterfalls and cascades. 4 The "arches" near Kamaishi, Iwate prefecture.

expect cafés and romantic fish restaurants down at the harbor.
Instead expect to see a gruesome tire factory with smoking stacks
and tall sea walls of steel and concrete surrounding even the love-
liest fishing village from the dreaded storm waves of the Pacific.
The other side of the main island, bordered by the Japanese Sea is
no less wild, rocky and bizarre. Sheer cliffs, roaring surf. Japan's has a
coastline almost 30,000 kilometers long, but the majority of it is wild
and ragged, so it is generally unsuitable for beach holidays. There are
few exceptions, namely the southern tropical islands of Okinawa.
Consequently Japan has hardly any coastal tourism. The Japanese do
not bathe in the sea (if this idea does occur to them they fly to
Guam or Hawaii). The Japanese prefer to soak in their hot natural
springs which are small and safe and without dangerous currents.

1 The onset of spring in the mountains, prefecture of Gunma. 2 View
from the foot of Mount Fuji: the mighty range of the Japanese Alps in
Yamanashi, west of Tokyo 3 Near Lake Akan in Hokkaido.

When General MacArthur decided to make Japan the "the Switzerland of Asia" after the Americans won the war in 1945, he didn't have to transplant any more mountains onto this island. You can safely view Japan as a single mountain range. There isn't a single spot in this country from where you can't catch a view of hills, mountains or entire mountain ranges in the distance on a clear day. There are the Japanese Alps with peaks over 3,000 meters high which are covered in snow from October right through to May. This presented quite a challenge to the highway engineers who had to excavate no less than 165 tunnels from the rock when they constructed the 1,300 kilometer stretch of highway, connecting Tokyo with the southern island of Kyushu. Some of these tunnels are only a few hundred meters long, others can extend up to eight kilometers. All in all at least 10 percent of the highway passes through tunnels.

Japan's "front", the highly developed, industrialized and completely built-up region faces the Pacific Ocean. The proud inhabitants of the Pacific region sometimes condescendingly refer to the other coast, which faces the Asian continent as ura-nihon – Japan's back, which can also be translated as "Japan's backside." Heading west from the main population centers Tokyo, Kawasaki and Yokohama, the next largest towns are: Nagoya, then Kyoto, Osaka and Kobe, finally Okayama and Hiroshima and the large cities of Kitakyushu and Fukuoka in northern Kyushu. Moving away from the coastal regions towards the interior, the population density and standard of development decrease quite rapidly and deserted canyons lie without a human trace. Even the range of the ubiquitous ringing noises is missing in this wilderness.

These regions and landscapes may seem like paradise for the traveler who's had enough of the large cities, but for the local people there is little that keeps them here. Whoever can will leave the area and seek his fortune, or at least find some work, in the large cities. The old people remain behind, often in pretty derelict houses or on run-down farms.

Prefectures such as Niigata and Yamaguta, Nagano and Gifu in central Japan or the prefecture of Tottori further west are terra incognita even for the Japanese from the coastal regions. If at all they are only known for their numerous bathing spots, the onsen with their hot springs. Other than that these areas are popular for the millions of hikers. The Japanese enjoy hiking almost as much as the Germans do. You'll find most of them on the smallest of the main islands, Shikoku. But here they don't hike for fun, here they are pilgrims dressed in white. They pay their respects to a total of 88 temples along a stretch of around 1,000 kilometers length, doing penance and ridding themselves of a worldly sin. Shikoku's topography is dramatic, too: mountains, canyons and only very little flat land.

And this is exactly what it looks like on Kyushu, the southernmost of the main Japanese islands. Kyushu is dominated and defined by the centrally located volcano Aso, a terrifying, bubbling gorge. It is

1 A terrifying, bubbling gorge: the volcano Aso in the heart of Kyushu.
2 Winter landscape in Gunma. 3 Pilgrims climbing the more than 700 steps of the Kotohira shrine in Shikoku.

The Sea of Japan conflict

The Sea of Japan extends from the west coast of Japan to the Asian continent, to be more precise to Korea. It has an approximate size of one million square kilometers and is 3,712 meters deep at its deepest point. The most important thing about the Japanese Sea is neither its rich fisheries, nor the beauty of its coastal landscape. If we are to believe the Japanese government, the most important thing about the Sea of Japan is its name. The Japanese government finds it

completely unacceptable that the Korean government would like to have this sea internationally known as the "East Sea". This is what it is called in Korea. Presumably as, seen from Korea, it lies to the east. But as it lies to the west of Japan, the name "East Sea" could create a lot of confusion. But the main issue here is that Japan would never cease using its name for a sea, least of all if it is being put under pressure by the Koreans to do so. Both nations dislike each other as much as say the French and the British. And so this ugly and in principal superfluous conflict gets washed to and fro between both countries on the sometimes gentle, sometimes rocky waves of the Sea of Japan and the Korean East Sea. As though this world didn't have enough of them already.

also home to many other active volcanoes, such as the Unzen-dake whose last eruption in May 1991 claimed 40 victims and the Sakura-jima which smokes impressively above the southern port town Kagoshima. And not far from there, at the southernmost tip of Kyushu, embedded in green tea plantations, you'll see the Kai-mon, the "Fuji of Kyushu" as this volcano is called. Its symmetrical cone is a small, 900 meter high, perfect replica of famous Fuji-san. There are more than 100 active volcanoes in Japan. Most of them are located in northern Honshu and in Hokkaido. We should have a closer look at the most famous one of them all. Luckily it has remained peaceful for the past 300 years…

Call of the Mountain
An excursion to Mount Fuji

With its height of 3,776 meters, Mount Fuji towers over all the other peaks of Japan. There's no other mountain in the world – neither Mount Olympus, nor the Matterhorn and not even Mount Everest – which even comes close to the way this mountain is instantly recognizable, as for its symbolic power, its aesthetic and artistic influence and its prolific use as a logo on t-shirts and mugs, fans and paintings.

There is no other natural scenery of their country that has so deeply and permanently impressed the Japanese as the symmetrical slopes of this holy mountain. This is shown in the works of the poets of the 8th century, the colorful woodcarvings of Hokusai (1760 – 1849) and on the steamed-up walls of every public bath. And it doesn't matter that the slopes aren't in fact all that symmetrical if you look closely from certain angles, for Mount Fuji has retained a rather ugly hump from its last eruption in 1707.

And there won't be another peak of its height in the world that has been climbed so often. During high season from July 1 to August 31, the fascinating Fuji attracts up to 300,000 mountaineers every year.

Mount Fuji lies less than 100 kilometers west of Tokyo. On clear days, which almost only occur in winter, its snow-capped peak can be seen from numerous vantage points in the city. These days, some people are looking at Fuji with a certain worry, for while its last eruption occurred 300 years ago, there is little reason why this volcano shouldn't start spewing fire and smoke again any time. The likely consequences would be that Tokyo would be covered by a blanket of ash 10 centimeters thick, the important national transport routes which all run past Fuji would be disrupted, public life in the capital would come to a standstill and the Japanese economy would collapse, at least temporarily.

As ghastly as these prospects are, the views of Mount Fuji are glorious from almost any angle, at any time of the year. There is one exception: the city of Fuji, an industrial center of almost grotesque ugliness, right at the foot of the mountain. More than 1,000 paper and chemical works and over 100 massive chimneystacks spoil the view and insult the eye. That's why the municipa-

1 One of the most popular views of Mount Fuji. 2 Volcano and ice – in winter the trees are turned into ice sculptures. 3 The Lake of Yamanaka, one of five Fuji lakes, is a popular destination for people wanting to take a break from the city. 4 One of the stunning works of art of the almost blind photographer Aikawa

lity has decided to subsidize the demolition of those stacks that are no longer needed. There is little as important and wonderfully uplifting to the Japanese as this: a good view of Mount Fuji.

The spooky Aokigahara Forest

Ever since Matsumoto Seicho, the master of murder mysteries, had a heartbroken district attorney and the defendant's wife commit suicide on the slopes of Mount Fuji in his novel "Nami-no-to" (The Tower of Waves) published in 1957, the Aokigahara Forest has been a popular destination for those weary of life. And there are disconcertingly many of them in Japan. The reasons for suicide include economic crises and companies going bust, fear of failure and feelings of shame. In 2002, there were more than 32,000 suicides!
And many are drawn to the spooky Aokigahara Forest for their

last desperate act. This forest is also referred to as "The Sea of Trees," where gnarly old trees cling onto sharp, craggy volcanic rock and where no compass works. Just in 2003 the neighboring commune Fuji-Yoshida salvaged 78 corpses in the forest during its grim annual search for them. Many had come from afar to commit suicide here. Maybe they were hoping to reach paradise quicker if they ended their lives here. A paradise where they aren't pursued and tortured by callous money lenders or cruel colleagues and bosses, a paradise where their unreciprocated love is returned or where they are not bowed down in shame for not being able to feed their family. In the restaurants and souvenir shops in the area, heart-breaking notes for help are pinned on the walls by people who have been looking for their nearest and dearest for weeks and months and who fear that this may have been their last stop. At the entry to the forest there are numerous signs that beg the suicidal wanderer to seek professional help. A specific hotline is offered, followed by the following appeal: "Your parents gave you your life. You cannot throw it away before you have spoken calmly with them, with your siblings and children once more."

1 Within seconds the cloud formations over Mount Fuji can change. **2** Almost every public bath in this country will have its walls adorned with a view of Mount Fuji. **3** On the shore of Lake Yamanaka.

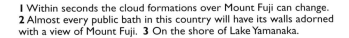

A life-long motive: the Fuji photographers

In this country of amateur photographers no motive is as coveted and sought after as Mount Fuji. It is the favorite motive of well-equipped hobby photographers who gather in full force on certain days and at certain strategic vantage points. That might be that on an April morning when the sun rises right above Fuji's peak. Such a strategic vantage point may be a place where a branch of a cherry tree in full blossom or particularly dense autumn leaves frame the mountain slopes particularly beautifully. Whoever failed setting up the tripod the night before will miss out come sunrise.

For some, such as for Mr. Aikawa Makoto, age 73, taking photographs of Mount Fuji – and only of Mount Fuji – has become a life-long project. Throughout the past 17 years he has taken photographs of nothing other than Japan's most beautiful volcano. In every light, at every time of the year, at any time of the day. "I am not interested in any other motive," he tells me. He and his wife have found at least 100 vantage points from which the view of the mountain is particularly

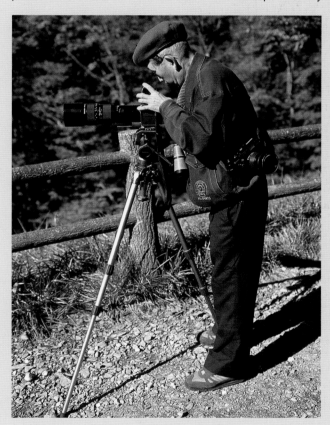

good. Some of them are right by the roadside; others can only be reached after a strenuous hike of several hours. That in itself would be impressive enough. But on top of that Mr. Aikawa is almost blind. He doesn't see the mountain with his eyes, but with his heart. He has a feeling for the particular light and his wife helps him focus his camera. With this method he has succeeded in taking the most wonderful pictures. He lent me one of them (see pages 28/29), so that you can see for yourself.

In the Land of Harmony
Enchanting manners

"These people refresh my soul", the Spanish Jesuit priest Francisco de Javier (also known as Francis Xavier) is said to have exclaimed. He arrived in Kagoshima, Kyushu, in 1549 as one of Japan's first visitors from the West. His mission was to convert the Japanese to Christianity. "My family and I could hardly believe that such wonderful people as the Japanese exist on our planet", a tourist, Stephen Hertel from Wisconsin, wrote in an enthusiastic letter to the "Japan Times" on May 5, 2004. Whatever it is that defines the Japanese, it is something that touches us "Westerners" deeply. Sometimes it almost enchants us. It is something that has worked for at least 450 years.

This element is best understood by someone who has lived in Japan for a while, returns home and misses it terribly: the general atmosphere of politeness, consideration and respect.

It is a feeling that we are not used to – that complete strangers actively make an effort not to hurt our feelings, not to expose us to their moods and not to bulldoze us with a potentially completely screwed-up ego and its associated problems. And they do so even though and especially because we look completely different, haven't got a clue about the language and tend to behave like bulls in a china store. The real culture shock comes after returning home after spending a while in Japan. A cranky customs official might bark at you for no reason whatsoever as soon as you arrive at the airport, the cab driver is crabby and maybe you'll have the pleasure of a stressed cashier the first time you enter a store. Just one of these individual experiences is usually sufficient for me to want to return to Japan as soon as possible. And I dare not think how it might make the Japanese feel, who, – surprisingly enough – are still coming over to visit us. I sometimes wish I could be there each time one of them is rudely woken up in our gruff world of bad manners for me to bow and say: *"Shitsurei-itashi-mashita –* someone has just lost his politeness here. Please do not take it personally – it's just the way we are…"

When a Japanese restaurant has not yet opened, there will be a sign telling you: "We are preparing." This is a friendly way of informing the potential customer that this restaurant is strictly speaking

1 Rock 'n' Roll as a way of life. 2 On "Coming-of-Age Day," the 20-year-olds make a pilgrimage to the shrine, dressed in their fur-collared kimonos. 3 Aja Kong – an infamous professional wrestler. 4 Blossom hostesses in Mito. In spring thousands of plum trees attract millions of visitors to this place.

not open yet, but that every effort is being made to open up soon. You won't find such a signs at the door of any of our restaurants in Western Europe. Here you are merely coolly informed about the opening hours: "From noon on – and not a minute earlier – you'll be able to eat here, you idiot. How dare you bother us this early?" Of course that is not the exact wording, but I am merely trying to convey what someone who has been influenced by the Japanese culture might read between the lines.

Or if you enter any store in Japan, even if it is a 24-hour store where you might buy a pack of chewing gum and a brush for the sum total of two fifty, you will also be greeted by a clear "irasshai-masse! – Welcome to our store!" And even if there was only one single person in front of you at the checkout, the cashier will say: "Omatase itashimashita! – I have left you, the honored customer, waiting. I am sorry." And when the clerk has parceled up the pack

of chewing gum and the hairbrush for you, you'll actually hear: "Thank you very much for visiting us. Please honor us again soon." Isn't that wonderful? Of course this is not meant literally. Most likely, the cashier couldn't care less about you. But these niceties are uttered anyways and that makes a small, but significant difference. How often do you encounter that sort of politeness at our checkouts at home? And isn't it nice if you don't even have to get out of your car at the gas station, but friendly, quick people not only fill up the tank for you, but also — only after they've asked for permission — proceed to clean your windshield and empty your ashtrays for you? Isn't that what we expect from a service society? I am reluctant to even start counting down the stupid and unfair

1 This friendly lady is selling snacks made of konyaku, a jelly-like substance made with the starch of yam roots. **2** Trade fair hostesses at the Tokyo Motor Show. **3** Even Samurai actors have to rest occasionally.

Mr. Kitahara's resistance

Mr. Kitahara Koji is the owner of a small fabric store in the little town of Narita which belongs to the prefecture of Chiba and is located about 60 kilometers from Tokyo. He is 84 years old and for

the past 40 years, he has been fighting the equally hopeless and bitter battle against Tokyo's International Airport. Mr. Kitahara is living evidence that the Japanese are capable of exceptional stub-

bornness and animosity towards the authorities, if they feel that their principals and rights have been violated and that they are being treated unfairly.

When the government decided to build a new airport in the mid 1960's, they selected the rice and vegetable fields of Narita as the new site. The affected farmers weren't consulted, as one probably assumed that they would feel privileged by this choice. But that wasn't the case at all. The farmers resisted strongly, were soon supported by radical students, and the construction of the airport turned into a long, tiring war between the police and the demonstrators. It went on for several years, resulting in deaths and injuries on both sides. To this day, all documents and luggage of every passenger are checked before they are even allowed to enter the terminal – this is how deep the trauma and fear of the anti-airport activists is. To this day, several farmers blankly refuse to sell their land, thus preventing the planned expansion of the airport. They calmly continue growing their organic vegetables while thundering jets fly overhead. If you look out of the airplane window during take-off or touch-down, you might be able to make out their placards saying: "Down with Narita Airport."

Mr. Kitahara is the leader of a particularly uncompromising wing of the enemies of the airport. As such he is always shadowed by plain-clothed policemen and his phone is bugged. He has declined millions, job offers and all the resettlement proposals of the government. "I will never give up," he says. "Everyone says Japan is a democracy. But they simply ignored our rights!" Japan's society is based on the philosophy of consensus and harmony. But these values don't fall from the sky; they are the result of hard work and lengthy negotiations. Whoever ignores the rules of consensus, such as the government did in its plans for Tokyo airport, will create bitter enemies for himself, even in the "nation of smiles."

prejudices towards the Japanese and the stereotypes into which they are squeezed. They range from the camera juggling, dumb tourist to the fanatical public servant who is at risk of killing himself by working too much, to the cool, intimidating super manager. And the worst thing is: Even at home in Japan the Japanese present a forum for the crudest critics and dimwits because for some unknown reason, they love to ponder their own idiosyncrasies and be misunderstood by outsiders. They love to shake their head about themselves and then simply continue in the same way they are used to. They present a stage for every fool who makes fun of them, ensuring that his books become bestsellers and his shows on TV attract millions. Why?

They simply find themselves amusing. They certainly don't need us to occasionally find themselves extremely funny. I have never met another nation that can laugh about itself in such a whole-hearted way. The Japanese relish the fact that they are something special. *"Wareware nihonjin – us Japanese…"* This means: us Japanese and the rest of the world. They are very keen on that concept and they are particularly interested in what the rest of the world thinks of them. There are not another people more open towards new ideas, recipes and fashions and one that can adopt them as easily. But they do not want to change. The way it should be.

1 Proud member of a matsuri, a religious feast. **2** Fish vendor in Tsukiji, the largest fish market in the world. **3** For the matsuri, small kids are also dressed up in traditional clothes. **4** Happy farmer on Miyako-Jima, Okinawa, harvesting sugar beet. **5** Organic farmer Onishi is especially proud of his huge beets.

Undoubtedly the Japanese have quite an image problem even on a worldwide scale. Amongst their Asian neighbors they are often admired, but in some countries they are truly hated. This applies particularly to the Chinese, who cannot forgive them for what Japan did to their country between 1937 and 1945. (This is something that the majority of Japanese stubbornly refuse to admit). In the West where not much is known about their country and society, they are considered at least strange, most probably unfathomable and dangerous in the worst case.

Our perception is that the Japanese bow a lot, constantly say 7 and continuously smile for no reason. At least the latter is true, for the Japanese are very friendly by nature. And throughout their long history in a relatively small space they have developed a most pleasant culture of dealing with each other. It is based in mutual respect and politeness and on the fact that they simply ignore people they don't know. Whoever might consider this amusing and silly deserves all the trouble he has with his next-door neighbor. Driving through the traffic of Tokyo, it is surprising to find that a car can be maneuvered through town without honking the horn and without threatening other drivers. This is not because there is no reason to honk your horn, but because it is impolite and crude and the Japanese try to avoid such excesses whenever possible. The only explanation I can find for this highly pleasant way of dealing with one another is the high population density, narrow crowds and lack of space. This forces everyone to ignore his fellow citizen and leave him be – even if he has parked his car in the middle of the street and is calmly reading the newspaper behind the steering wheel.

Mr. Nishida survived

On August 9, 1945 Mr. Nishida Hideo was working in Mitsubishi's subterranean torpedo factory in his home town Nagasaki just like on any other day. That morning, the atom bomb exploded right above where he lives, in the densely populated part of town called Urakami. This part of Nagasaki is home to

the largest Christian community of Japan. Mr Nishida is a Christian himself. He described how there were corpses everywhere, all around. You could hardly walk a step without treading on one. Some of them looked like burnt trees from afar, with their arms spread out gruesomely, as though they were praying for help. It took him all day to find his way home through the completely destroyed town. That evening he found the ruins of his father's house. Over the course of the next days all his seven siblings died as a result of the nuclear radiation. Mr. Nishida told me that, although they couldn't understand why God was punishing them so, the Christians of Nagasaki immediately joined forces and built a new church, even before they started to rebuild their houses again. To this day, despite his 84 years, Mr. Nishida goes to early mass at the Urakami church at 6 o'clock every morning.

1. The dried seagrass of Shimoda is cherished for breakfast throughout Japan. 2. An injured hero who fell off the tree trunk at the Onbashira-Matsuri (see page 167). 3 Cheerful Sushi cook. 4 Fisher on the Izu peninsula.

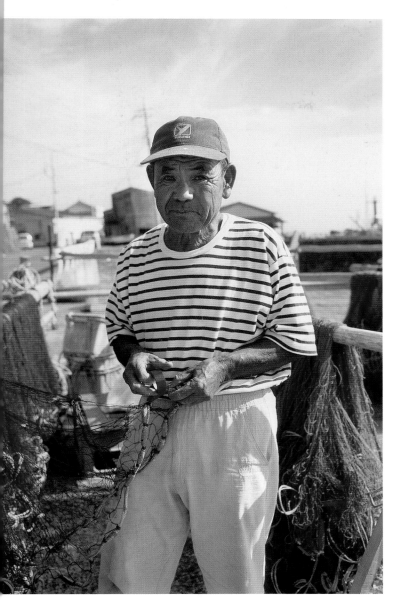

Happiness in old age: Mrs. Okushima

Mrs. Okushima Ushi is 100 years of age, perfectly healthy and energetic. Her secret is to rise with the chickens and to walk down to the nearby beach to do her morning exercises. Before going to bed she drinks a few glasses of sweet, hundred percent wormwood liqueur. Mrs. Okushima lives in the small village of Ogimi in the north of Okinawa. This is the place in Japan with the highest percentage of 100-year olds. Since many years Japanese women have enjoyed the leading

position as oldest women world-wide, with an average age of 85 years, whilst the Japanese men (average age 78 years) take the second prize behind the vivacious Hong Kong males. Researches believe that their diet is the reason for the longerity of the inhabitants of Ogimi. They use little salt, eat three times more vegetables than in northern Japan, eat significantly more tofu plus nutritious and very fatty pork. But, apart from their diet, experts acknowledge that the extremely warm and open nature of the people of Okinawa plus the fact that old people are not isolated here, but continue working, contribute to decisions, join in celebrations and partake in village life, are just as important for a long, healthy life.

In Ogimi every third person is over 65. For every person with a job there is a retired person who needs support. No country in the world ages faster than Japan. Already today 19 percent of the population is over 65 years of age, the birth rate is dropping steadily and, similar to the western world, nobody knows how this should all be financed in future. In any case, the stream of national and international visitors to Ogimi, the realm the happy old people, persists.

Everyone seems well aware that he or she might be in that same position one day.

Of course the Japanese are no better people than we are. Some of them are quite incredibly stubborn. Some, frequently those clad in expensive suits or uniforms, can be painfully arrogant. Others are amazingly submissive and many have the ugly tendency to be racist. Again others fiddle with their tax declaration, do not pick up litter they have dropped or commit violent crimes. This only serves to show that there is absolutely no point talking about "the Japanese" in general, to like "the Japanese," or to dislike, admire, be afraid of, despise or belittle "the Japanese."

And finally I guarantee you this: None of us would want to and would be able to submit to the crushing pressures of Japanese society, as much as we love these people and their gentle manners.

Girls, Manga, Costumes
Kosupuree – The youth is playing dress-up

Sometimes it appears as though some of the Japanese space ship crew has already bid good-bye to worldly reality and decided to live life as another sequel of the extremely popular Manga comics. Observers will get this feeling mainly on the weekends, when the kosupuree community assembles in certain urban parks. *Kosupuree* – derived from the English word costume play – means fancy dress and provides young people with the opportunity to briefly escape from their stressful everyday life, to break out of the corset of performance pressure at school and the constraints of society. An escape from nagging parents, stupid superiors and cruel teachers. But it also illustrates the desire of the Japanese to overstep all boundaries of good taste without being punished – at least in a confined place for a confined period of time.

For the kosupuree, young people happily slip into costumes, which they've usually tailored themselves with a lot of effort, and adopt a different identity. They pose as more or less magic dream figures: as princesses, space heroes and villains, as bunnies, hobbits or as Heidi. Among the more popular impersonations are that of a nurse with a bloody eye patch and vampire teeth, a female concentration camp guard with chains and armbands adorned with swastikas and doll-like frilly dresses in pink or pale blue, complete with a bonnet, corkscrew curls and lots of ribbons.

On the surface, kosupuree seems picturesque and exotic. To a transient it may seem like the colorful protest of a suppressed youth that must endure any kind of bullying during the week while nodding politely, so it has the urge to let off steam at the weekend. And you'll hardly find more colorful photo motives in the whole wide world. But please do not forget to ask before you take a picture – it is the polite thing to do. And that's precisely the point.

If you look closely, a strange and somehow spooky symbiotic relationship will reveal itself between those in fancy dress and the photographers. Those in fancy dress are mainly schoolgirls and young women who might have problems being accepted at work and amongst their friends. The photographers on the other hand are usually grown-up men or young men with perhaps even more hampered social skills that go hunting with their cameras and hide behind them. They have albums full of photographs of these,

1 Corkscrew curls and bonnets – a popular motive at the big kosupuree events. **2** Super heroes in their homemade space suits. **3** The "cruel" nurses hope you get better soon. **4** Many hundreds appear in costumes to pose in front of the camera.

let's say, unhappy girls who are willing to adopt any pose, be it child-like or lascivious, put them onto the Internet and show off with them.

Despite its incredible colors, eccentricity and superficial exuberance, such a kosupuree event is like a bizarre, sad dance of the inhibited and of those who have missed out. Without real joy and pleasure. Well, that's the way I felt anyway. That despite the fact that there is a lot of laughter, but usually, it's far too loud. And even though many make peace signs and lots of aspects seem to prove that Japan has lost it long term, as part of its youth has lost it. But I bet my bottom dollar that the kosupuree will infect our youth, too, in the wake of manga and computer games.

To me the kosupuree seemed more like a compulsive ritual based on the desperate need of girls for more attention, wanting to be desired models and stars – if even just for one day, for one photo– and the drooling curiosity of lecherous older men. If you want to experience rude, unfriendly and aggressive Japanese, just try to take pictures of the photographers themselves, instead of their models that are usually still school children. Those photog-

raphers queuing up to take a photograph of a desirable in a provocative pose to add these photographs to their own archives or websites. They know damn well that their photographs are not created for purely artistic reasons, but mainly for dirty motives. Yet you'll probably be most appalled when trying to speak to the creatures who are slightly taller than the others, those entirely covered by masks, flesh-colored t-shirts and stockings. For they won't answer, at best through a written reply. Many of those dressed in the costumes of popular Manga heroines are indeed young men.

1 For every "beauty"… **2** …there is always a "beast". **3** Please wait for your turn for a short photo session with the most desired models. **4** Masks offer first opportunities for kids to escape, too. **5** Normal clothes are brought along in suitcases. **6** Every girl has her own pose. **7** Space patrol – a popular manga series. **8** This young man handed me a written note that he likes small kids very much.

Japan hidden behind a mask

The urge to hide behind a mask occasionally, to adopt a different identity— although this identity is strictly defined and doesn't leave much creative freedom— and thus escape the strict rules of everyday life is something has been known since the 6th century, when the first masks appeared in Japan. Masks made of wood, lacquer, paper or clay are an important feature of art forms, of dance and religion. The *Noh* theater uses a stock of no less than 200 different masks. Nowadays this old tradition has been enriched with numerous motives from the world of Mickey Mouse, Hello Kitty, Winnie-the-Pooh and various super heroes. Masks are extremely popular and you won't come across any shrine festival or fun fair without a crowd of whining children around the colorful stall of the mask vendor.

Gel Massages for Zuzu
Kawaii! – The Japanese and their animals

Ｉn western countries, like your own, dogs were always useful. They were either used as hunting dogs, guard dogs or were needed to herd the sheep. In Japan we don't have this tradition," explains psychiatrist Dr.Sakai Kazuo when I asked him to give me a deep psychological explanation for Japan's incredible love for dogs. "Here in Japan our dogs don't have to work. Their sole purpose is to be loved and cuddled…"

Not only are dogs not required to work in Japan – most of them don't even need to walk. Prettified with colorful ribbons they are either transported in a bag or else master or mistress carries them in their arms. And you don't need complicated psychology to recognize that Chihuahuas, pugs and dachshunds are like substitute children for many urbanites. While Japan's birth rate is decreasing alarmingly and there will only be 100 million Japanese in the year 2050 (instead of 127 million as there are now), the number of registered and thoroughbred dogs has almost doubled between 1990 and 2002 up to a total of 537,648 registered dogs. In the same space of time the number of dog-breeds found in Japan increased from 106 to 149. In what kind of world can dog owners sue their vet for 33,000 euros in damages, claiming that their nine-year-old Pomeranian had died because the vet hadn't treated its diabetes correctly? In what kind of world can industry expect an annual turnover of around seven billion euros for pet care, such as anti-ageing skin cream and dog food made of organic vegetables? For artistic dog dishes, for anti-allergenic dog shampoo and an endless array of T-shirts, little shirts, panties and suits? Of course there are already hotels, cafés, restaurants, fitness studios and hairdressers for dogs. Recently a spa for dogs opened up in Tokyo– complete with wet gel massages for the neurotic dachshund and hot relaxing baths. In the lobby there's a clairvoyant for dogs who'll predict Zuzu's future.

"Kawaii" – is the jubilant cry and also the curse of modern Japan. Kawaii means as much as "sweet, cute" and it is the battle cry – mostly uttered in a semi-hysterical falsetto – by an entire generation that grew up with Hello Kitty and considers Mickey Mouse and Moncchichi dolls cultural achievements. It is a generation looking desperately for something cute to cuddle. Preferably something

1 Flock of suspicious ravens. 2 Cats are smart fashion accessories, best worn when running errands in town. 3 Sad bear prison in Hokkaido. 4 Handbag-sized dogs are most popular.

Dr. Hashiguchi's sand sauna

The vet Dr. Hashiguchi supports the hypothesis that what-ever is good for humans cannot harm an animal. He is one of those charming dropouts and individualists found regu-larly in Japan's supposedly uniform society. The animal lover Dr. Hashiguchi quit his job at the University of Tokyo and has been cruising around in a bus converted into an animal clinic through the picturesque landscape of the southern Kyushu peninsula ever since. Here he treats his furry patients with the presumably wholesome sand sauna for which the beaches of the nearby small town of Ibusuki have become well known throughout the country. Dr. Hashiguchi wraps the

animals lovingly in a hemp sack and buries them in the hot sand – right up to their necks. Apparently it helps cure skin diseases and gets rid of parasites. And a beneficial side effect: It relaxes any creature. Therefore this treatment is also recommended for hyper-nervous and neurotic dogs – and which animal living Japanese dog's life wouldn't become one?

1 Deer live in the temple districts of the old capital city Nara and enjoy serious conversations with the tourists. **2** It is debatable whether this dog is really enjoying his bath. **3** Mummy always has a tit-bit ready. **4** The traditional monkey show. **5** The fox as messenger of the gods – found at every Shinto shrine. **6** The badger as a cheerful drinker – a symbol of hospitality.

that can wear pink and has big, sad, black eyes. This phenomenon doesn't frighten me because it is so prevalent in Japan, but because it will most likely also crop up in Europe as well eventually, thanks to globalization and the universal rules of post-industrial society. The Japanese are not strange and eccentric – they are simply a few steps ahead of us in certain areas.

With the battle cry "kawaii," even elderly ladies pounce on a ferret on a leash or join the grateful audience of the traveling monkey shows that have entertained visitors to the temples and shrines since medieval times. "Saru-mawashi," the old art of training macaques, is widespread even in modern-day Japan. It is part of the tradition of training animals to imitate human behavior to evoke laughter, a thrilled "kawaii" and a murmur of amazement.

Animals have a firm place in Japan's long history, its myths and its treasure of legends. Often creatures such as monkeys, foxes and crows are viewed as messengers of the gods. Illustrations of animals belong to religious life – you will find sculptures of foxes at every Shinto shrine. Since ancient times, foxes were thought to be able to put a spell on humans. (This belief, like many others, most likely originated in China where the spirit of the fox is feared as a tricky cheater.) The tanuki, the badger or raccoon, is believed to hold similar powers, apart from being an entertainer. Semi-sweet

semi-ugly clay sculptures of this creature will welcome you in front of many restaurants. Complete with a straw hat, a sake jug and a large belly it is supposed to create an image of jolly joie-de-vivre. And the maneki-neko, the ubiquitous welcoming cat with its raised right paw will be right next to it. Maneki-neko is supposed to bring business success and happiness to a restaurant or a store. The Japanese deer (shika) are holy animals in the Shinto religion. They roam around parks, such as on the island of Miyajima or particularly in the ancient capital Nara.

The almost vanished natives of Hokkaido, the Ainu, revered the abovementioned as deities. The kind of bears they encountered were the frightening higuma – relatives of the North American Grizzly. The climax of their religious life was the bear feast where a bear that had been raised in the village was honored for three days. Representing its kind, the animal was given thanks for his fur and meat. At the end of the feast the bear was strangled ritually to be able to rise straight to bear paradise. Beyond its expansive forests, Hokkaido is anything but a bear paradise nowadays, however. A ritual strangling would probably mean mercy for the pitiful creatures in the various "bear parks" on the island, where they are trained to pedal around on bikes wearing little skirts and spend a sad life in dirty cages or enclosures made of concrete.

Since ancient times crows were also considered messengers of the gods and— for reasons I cannot fathom— the crow is the heraldic animal of the Japanese football association. They represent Tokyo's main terror, apart from the loudspeaker announcements and ringing tones. At closer look, Tokyo's crows are in fact large ravens with horrible, very sharp beaks. Their sight is quite intimidating, tempting you to cross over to the other side of the street. Up to 30,000 of these feathered hooligans inhabit Japan's capital city and their cawing represents the early morning concert, especially on days when the garbage is being collected. Japan doesn't believe in garbage containers – mainly because there truly is no room for them in the narrow streets – but gets rid of garbage in plastic bags that are piled up at the various collection points. Naturally, greedy beaks easily hack up these plastic bags and a clan of crows devours the remains of the spaghetti from the previous evening. As soon as they've finished, they'll fly in flocks to the nearest balcony and steal the wire clothes hangers from the bamboo washing poles– which the lady of the house has just bought from the loud traveling bamboo washing pole man – because wire clothes hangers are their preferred material for nest building. A crow carrying a clothes hanger,

a piece of toast or even a bottle of mayonnaise, a particular treat for crows, is no rare sight in Tokyo.

Japan's most valued creature (in terms of the price people are willing to pay for it) is the blessedly silent and noble *koi*, the ornamental carp. According to a Chinese legend, a carp once swam up a river and turned into a dragon. Ever since this fish has been a symbol of success. Around May 5 of each year, on the "Day of Children", proud parents throughout the country raise the colorful carp flags *(koi-nobori)* to express their hope that their sons will succeed in life. A Japanese dream of earthly wealth will possibly include a Ferrari, but will certainly include a garden pond with several of these splendid ornamental fishes swimming around in it majestically. Here in the west, the koi aesthetics, in parallel with the breakthrough of Sushi, has long prevailed.

And although the prices for these fish with their attractive patterns, bright colors and streamlined shape have dropped since the

1 Tokyo's ravens attacking the garbage in the morning. **2** Koi – the equivalent of a sports car as a fish in a pond. **3** Expert assessment of the winner of the national koi competition. **4** Koi-nobori, the carp flags blowing in the wind throughout the country in springtime.

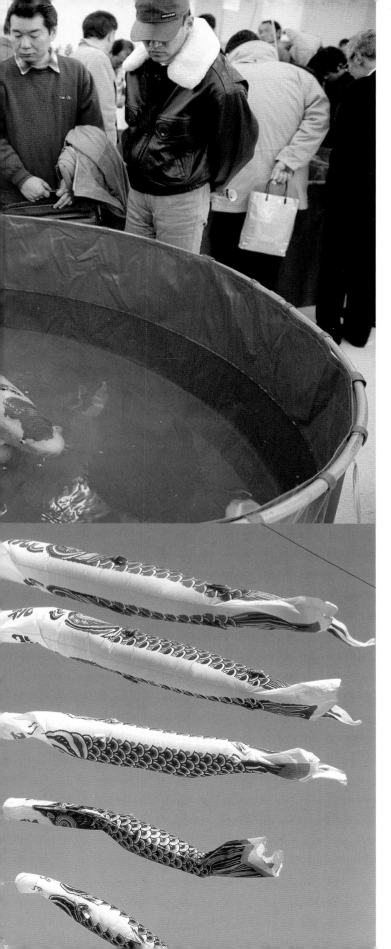

Beloved nuisances

Even insects are revered with almost cultic enthusiasm. Among them is the stag beetle whose headgear reminds the historically educated entomologist of Samurai armor. Yet the real queen of the bugs is the semi, the Japanese cicada, which appears after the rainy season in the oppressive heat of the summer. Forget everything you have heard during your travels in southern countries. Imagine a guy with a power saw sitting in the cherry tree next to your bedroom. And imagine that his job starts at sunrise, at the ungodly hour of around 5 am. I have no idea how these insects the size of my thumb manage to generate so much noise, but the result is deafening! The following few noticeable lines escaped from the great Japanese poet Basho's pen in the 17th century: "Stillness. The song of the semi penetrates the rock". The Japanese are

not bothered by the cacophony of snoring, rasping and sawing. On the contrary, they love their semi, as this creature embodies one of their romantic ideals. They lie dormant in the earth for many years, then pupate for just a few days, generate an incredible ruckus, reproduce and then die. For a nation so in love with the transitory and which has elevated brave endurance in the face of overwhelming obstacles to a kind of religion, these semi are admirable nuisances with a supreme symbolic power.

golden 80's of the 20th century, when immense sums of money were paid – occasionally as much as around 300,000 euros – the award-winning super fish that are determined during the huge show of the Japanese koi breeder association every year, are worth their weight in gold. More often than not quite a bit more…

Be Very Prepared
The next earthquake is bound to hit

Incidentally, an animal is responsible for earthquakes according to ancient beliefs: The Edo contemporaries of medieval times imagined that there was a big catfish dwelling somewhere beneath the earth that made the world tremble whenever it moved. And even though there now are more plausible scientific explanations for the phenomenon, it is one hard fact of Japan that is hard to accept: It occasionally starts to shake incredibly without prior warning. Unfortunately, Japan is located right on top of where three tectonic plates — the Asian, the Pacific and the Philippine plates — meet and the country is literally ripped apart by opposing tectonic movements. In the long-term — fortunately the very long-term — this will result in the entire nation eventually disappearing into the sea. These days it just trembles. Without ceasing. The fine sensors buried throughout the country pick up around 100,000 tremors annually. Of these, around 1,000 are felt by humans. I estimate, for example, that people in Tokyo get a real scare around 30 times during an average year, when they ask themselves: Oh no…is this the real thing now…?!

The small tremors, size 1 or 2 on the Japanese scale, are soft and almost playful. The maximum they do is provoke the question: "Did you feel that?" and the answer: "No, what?" And if they occur at night, they only wake up the particularly sensitive sleepers. Size 3 scares everybody, however, and leads to a disconcerting creaking of houses. During size 4, your cupboard doors will rattle. Size 5 will add to this drama and result in the doors banging, the glasses in the cupboard rattling, pictures on the wall starting to swing and residents will nervously look around for the sturdy dinner table or the doorframes. It is recommended to quickly hide under them, should scale size 6 or 7 hit.

No matter what the tremor size, one should quickly switch on the TV, as all channels will show an earthquake warning within seconds. Within minutes, the government-owned channel NHK will present accurate information on the magnitude and the epicenter and answer the most vital question to coastal communities: Is there a risk of a *tsunami,* a storm wave?

Earthquakes never tend to occur when you are prepared. Or when sitting on a huge meadow with nothing above to fall on your head and kill you. Earthquakes typically occur when you're lying in

1 Volunteer helpers salvaging a victim. **2** Shock at the press of a button — a family being shaken about in a simulator. **3** Roll call for the disaster drill **4** More than 6,000 people died in the Kobe earthquake in 1995.

your bathtub, enjoying an appointment at your dentist, sitting in your car, in a traffic jam on a bridge, or when you're somewhere up high trying to enjoy the view. This is why all experts agree: Always be prepared and expect anything to happen. But this can get very tiring and when nothing happens for weeks on end, it is all too tempting to feel much too safe again.

The Japanese use their enviable capacity of selective perception to also just ignore the threat of earthquakes. Shigata-ga nai – there's nothing that can be done about it. Although regular emergency drills take place, particularly on September 1 – the annual nation-wide earthquake preparation day plus the anniversary of the great Kanto earthquake in 1923, where around 140,000 people died – nobody really believes that a big earthquake will happen. Even though everyone should be aware by now that in the event of a large earthquake, thousands of people will die in Tokyo and every-thing will break down. The authorities generously concede that they will need at least three to four days to become functional again and that every survivor will have to fend for himself or her-self during this time.

No water, no electricity, no phone lines. The traffic will come to a complete standstill, nothing to eat or drink. Fires are everywhere,

without any fire brigade in sight. That is the horror scenario of a large earthquake in Tokyo.

After the large Kobe earthquake in 1995, only two percent of the injured and buried were brought to safety by rescue teams. Indeed, 98 percent were saved by their families, friends and neighbors. For that reason, there are volunteers in every district: People will have to rely on their neighborhood for help. These volunteers are prim-arily elderly citizens, retirees such as Mr. Ishiyama, a former head-master with his 26 co-volunteers in the district of Arakawa in Tokyo's east. Mr. Ishiyama Mitsuo is 80 years of age and he some-times sleeps fully clothed to be prepared. This is how seriously he takes his responsibility. Every couple of months the men and women get together and practice the emergency routines. They carry injured people out of their houses on their backs and free buried people with chain saws, test their life nets handmade from anti-crow nets and also render first aid. In the meantime, the women cook up emergency rations of vegetable rice. In a real emergency, hundreds of neighbors will be dependent on their help – especially young people who like to shirk participation in these drills. They can sleep soundly because Mr. Ishiyama is in bed with his clothes on, looking after them.

Alarm in the zoo!

In the midst of the cruelty and arbitrariness of the forces of nature, it is admirable how the Japanese always try to see the funny side of even the grimmest of reality. One of the most dramatic and humorous climaxes of the year are the emergency drills which are held in turn by the two large zoos of the capital, Ueno and Tama. For this purpose a staff member is stuck into an animal costume. This time it hits Ms. Sakai from the Insect House, who has to get dressed up as a snow leopard. The scenario is hair-raising: The cage sprang open

during an earthquake and the bloodthirsty wild animal is freely roaming the zoo. For the purpose of the exercise, a group of a hundred firemen, assistant police and zoo guards have gathered, armed with water guns, walkie-talkies, nets and rifles with ammunition to tranquilize the animal. They assemble at the deer enclosure where the showdown with the escaped wild cat is planned. Mrs. Sakai, who is sweating profusely and can hardly breathe in her cute costume, is linked to someone guiding her via walkie-talkie as she can hardly see a thing. She starts to stagger along, followed by cheerful, laughing camera teams and press photographers. Occasionally, she lifts her arms, which is supposed to look threatening, but only serves to delight the gaggle of people from the press. It is hard to say whether she responds to the invitation of one of the camera guys to growl, for the thick fur of her costume swallows any sound. It takes her around half an hour for the 300-meter stretch to the deer enclosure. Here she is quickly surrounded by helmet-wearers who spread a net around her and splashed with water from the water gun, which moistens the ground. While the pursuit vehicle with the tranquilizer shooter gets stuck in the mud, Ms. Sakai seriously injures an imprudent emergency helper by biting and scratching him. The situation seems to get out of control. In the end, the beast is overpowered; a shot from the tranquilizing gun and it starts to sway, slowly collapses and is finally wrapped up in the net and lifted onto the pick-up.

The deep seriousness with which everyone participates in this exercise raises the suspicion that they are all having a great time.

1 School children at one of their regular evacuation exercises. **2** A sand sack is used to test the self-made life net. **3** The women are in charge of the emergency provisions. **4** Mr. Ishiyama is the earthquake representative and the eldest of his district.

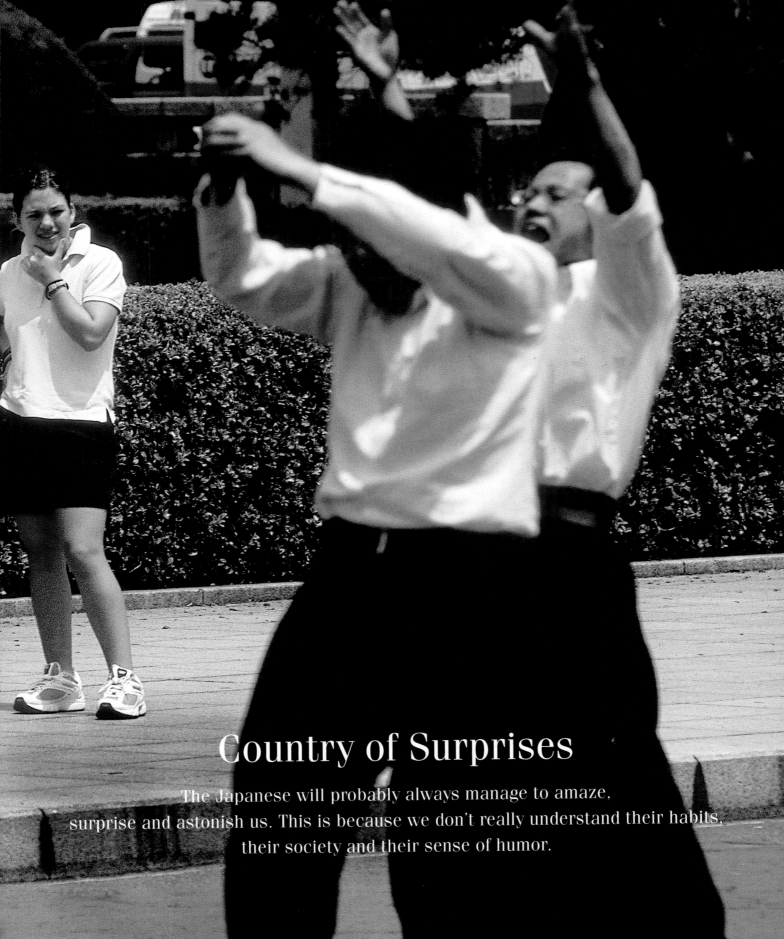

Country of Surprises

The Japanese will probably always manage to amaze, surprise and astonish us. This is because we don't really understand their habits, their society and their sense of humor.

In Between Tatami Mats and Giant Spiders
Living in Japan

et's begin by allowing ourselves to be a little amazed as to how the Japanese live.

There is no other structure which is better suited to the oppressive heat of Japanese summer than the traditional Japanese house. It is made of wood with sliding doors which can be removed to let in a cool breeze. The porch extends into the garden seamlessly, as the Japanese consider the house and garden as a unit. This would be the ideal Japanese house and occasionally you'll still find one – however usually only in open-air museums. The invention of the air conditioner, which is a "must" in even the most basic apartment, has rendered the traditional way of constructing houses obsolete. On top of that, whilst the old houses may have been lovely and breezy in summer, they would have been horribly draughty and cold in winter.

The Japanese farmhouses with their roofs thickly thatched with reed are much more suited to the cold. They are the typical farmhouse of the other side of the mountains in the west, near the coast of the Sea of Japan and in those regions affected by the Siberian cold. They were cozy and warm inside, even when the temperatures dropped dramatically, but on the other hand they were also very dark. It is hard to imagine how people could live in them without rushing outside every few minutes to escape the suffocating smoke from the open fireplaces. These days, these houses, too, are almost only found in special reserves, whilst the majority of the rural population lives in frequently very drab modern houses with blue sheet metal roofs. On the completely built-up plains and along the coasts with their walls of concrete, you'll really have to look very hard to find a "pretty" village which appeals to our Western taste.

The cities, too, offer only few optical highlights. Even the old emperor city Kyoto, whose historical center was destroyed in an almost criminal way in the 1960's, only boasts a few remaining streets lined with houses with traditional wooden fronts, creating the breeze of a pleasant atmosphere. These few old streets are found in the "Geisha quarter" Gion. In general the Japanese have a completely different feeling for what creates a nice atmosphere to us. There is no other way to justify the horrible lighting in their offices,

1 The ideal Japanese house – unfortunately very rare. **2** Reed-thatched roofs were common in the past, mainly in the countryside. **3** The notorious "golden flame" on the roof of a brewery. **4** Roppongi Hills, Tokyo's latest architectural achievement.

Experiments

Thanks to the almost complete absence of strict regulations and concepts with regard to urban construction and design, builders and architects have almost limitless creative freedom. I want to present just three examples of their playful pleasure of creating monstrosities. First of all the "golden

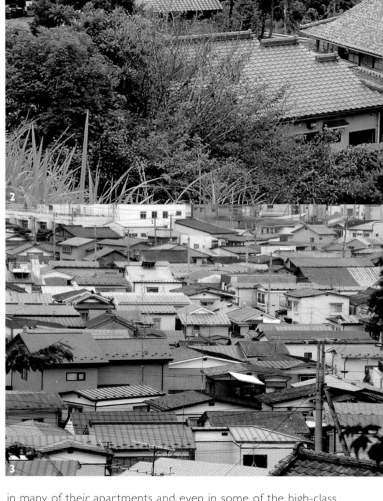

flame" at the headquarters of the Asahi brewery. It is also referred to as the "golden peanut". Those with a sense for the drastic also refer to it as the "golden...". Just a few streets away the gigantic French-looking chef presides over Kappabashi, the specialist area for the needs of restaurants and caterers. And finally the large spider at the entrance of the new Mori building in Roppongi is worth a mention. The property giant Mori wants to raise public awareness of the avantgarde with this piece of art and wants to attract support for his project – to demolish all of Tokyo and reconstruct it again.

in many of their apartments and even in some of the high-class *ryokan* (traditional inns). They use merciless, cold fluorescent lighting all over the place.

In the cities, terrace houses built along streets full of busy open warehouses were always the preferred homes. Here, too, wood

1 Kumamoto castle with its massive walls. 2 The ideal Japanese village framed idyllically by fields and hills – there aren't many of them left. 3 Not much space – a settlement on the Pacific coast in northern Honshu. 4 One house next to another in Yanaka, one of Tokyo's districts. 5 Not much is left of old Kyoto – almost only the "Geisha quarter" in Gion. 6 Old country house of the famous "Heike" family in Shikoku.

was the favored construction material. On the one hand this provided a certain amount of protection during earthquakes, but on the other it also resulted in whole parts of town regularly burning to the ground. In the past, only the warehouses were made of stone. Stones were also used for the bases of the castles which the military leaders erected, as well as for the huge walls which surrounded them. The castles themselves were naturally made of wood. Therefore they also burnt down at some stage. Most castles that you can visit today were reconstructed after World War II.

Japanese cities look uncannily similar and often look as though they have been randomly assembled from hundreds of different building sets. They are convoluted, without any recognizable overall concept. They seem to have sprawled wildly, rather than grown. The first thing the European visitor, who is spoilt with old cities and pedestrian zones back home, will probably notice is the complete absence of a cozy ambience which only old houses can create. But although old houses may be lovely to look at, they are impractical, and their substance is often rotten. They are drafty inside, but the owners are usually unwilling to do something about that, as it would cost a fortune to insulate and renovate them. Renovation isn't a concept in this country of fires, landslides, earthquakes and

庫　港運　会社

Façades – between traditional and hyper-modern: **1** Bast blinds, greenery and slanted roofs... **2** ...wooden façades... **3** ...and sliding doors covered with paper create a unique atmosphere. **4** Transparent luxury design – the prestigious "Prada" building in Tokyo's district Aoyama. **5** Apartments with a view of the city highway. **6** A warehouse in Otaru, Hokkaido. **7** Noodle

other natural disasters. Anything old is usually demolished and replaced with the consent of all. Also, inheritance tax is extremely high and has to be paid immediately. This is enough reason for even the nicest, most loyal heir to quickly sell his parental home to a property speculator who will immediately flatten and divide the property up into plots for five new houses or for a neat apartment building containing at least 15 apartments.

There are hardly any building regulations. One of the few stipulates that a new house which is constructed on a street of similar houses may only be a certain bit higher and may not reduce the amount of light the neighbors receive. This explains the pyramid-like silhouettes you often see. Apart from that, modern Japanese architects don't accept any taboos and don't shy away from experimenting with all kinds of exotic add-ons either.

The village of Shirakawago: **1** The traditional houses are built generously and are thickly thatched to keep out the cold. **2** The fireplace is in the center of the rural living room. **3** Narrow roads, little space – in mountainous Japan people always had to huddle closely together.

2

Standard measurement of living

The *tatami* mat, the floor cover of traditional houses ever since the ninth century, is a frame filled with rice straw, covered with rushes and tightly bound by a firm braid. Up to this day it is a standard for any Japanese apartment, even if

the floor has already been covered by carpeting or laminate as is the case with most new apartment buildings. But even brand-new apartments have at least one *tatami* room for special occasions. In Tokyo the standard *tatami* mat measures 176 x 88 cm. In Kyoto and Nagasaki it is a little larger. The good, real *tatamis* are made by hand by specialists. Then they are fitted into the rooms and can be turned around after a few years when the sunlight has bleached them. When both sides of the *tatami* mat are worn out, they simply receive a new cover. The floors of temples, shrines and prayer halls, and of many restaurants and assembly rooms, are covered with these rice straw mats. Of course they are ruined if you walk on them with shoes or if you put heavy furniture on them.

Nature in a Straitjacket

Heroes and rebels of the art of gardening

In Japan, gardens were always the privilege of the nobles, the class of warriors. They were strict people whose militant profession alone prevented two thoughts from occurring to them. Namely: why not leave nature up to chance – just a teeny bit? And: why not allow nature to deviate just a fraction from the ideal? They were very aware of hierarchies, obsessed with form and certainly not in the mood for experiments. The strictly structured Japanese gardens, their little landscapes including their stylized bridges, pagodas and lanterns, their mountains and coasts represent no less than the basic mentality of discipline, order and subordination translated into garden language.

There are strict rules, defined by old masters, for everything in a Japanese garden. Exceptions and individual wishes are not acceptable. This also applies to the Japan's horticultural icons, Bonsai and Ikebana, which, if you look closely, are nothing else but the submission of nature to human will and ideals in accordance with strict formalities. I think many Japanese people cannot really grasp the concept of natural wilderness, although their adoration of nature is praised again and again. The lack of order and the arbitrariness of uncontrolled nature frightens and intimidates them. This may be the reason why they haven't been looking after the natural environment of their magnificent islands particularly well, particularly in modern times. There is nothing that bothers a Japanese gardener more than dry leaves on the ground and branches sticking out haphazardly.

On the other hand, to be fair, I need to add that you keep on meeting adventurous Japanese who adore trekking through the wildest and highest mountains and don't shy away from even the steepest trails through the darkest forests, even if there's a sign warning them "Beware of the bears!" Is that paradoxical? No. You simply cannot make general statements about what "the Japanese" are like. Let's finally move away from clichés!

In any case the traditional Japanese garden hasn't got much to do with nature. But on the other hand, there are very few gardens which captivate visitors as much, provided they are open to the experience.

1 We put plants on our balconies. The Japanese put plants in front of their door. 2 Stone garden, Silver Pavilion, Kyoto. 3 True heroes of the art of gardening quickly take over the sidewalks. 4 The Zen garden in the Ryoanji Temple needs to be raked every morning.

As opposed to those of us who tend to feel restless after a few minutes (or maybe that only applies to me), the Japanese are able to spend hours letting their eyes wander across the groomed landscape of an expertly installed garden, completely entranced, drinking green tea. The pleasure of a garden and a cup of tea are intricately linked together. Consequently a tea house is a "must" in every larger garden and in any garden worth its name.

The so-called Muromachi period (1333–1568) is considered the "golden period" of the great Japanese art of gardening. This period was marked by enormous unrests, but also by large artistic devel-

1 Fall mood at the Jingo-Ji temple in an outlying district of Kyoto. **2** The garden becomes one with the surrounding landscape. **3** The enjoyment of gardens and the enjoyment of tea belong together – the tea house in Suizen-ji park in Kuamamoto. **4** Tea break with a view over the garden at the Shanzen-in temple, Kyoto.

opments. Professional garden architects traveled across the country, pursuing their vision of creating the universe in a small space, even just symbolically. They tried to create miniature replicas of famous landscapes and historically significant settings by arranging stones or sand like cliffs and oceans, but always bearing in mind that the surrounding landscape is part of the garden view. The shape of the garden was ideally supposed to be echoed by the natural mountain ranges and coasts.

The most famous example of this is the Suizenji park in Kumamoto where the artist reproduced 53 stations of the Tokaido Road which ran from Kyoto to Edo (the former Tokyo) – complete with a Fuji-san of five meters height.

A magnificent garden scene inspired by Buddhism developed alongside the art of gardening of the warriors. Incidentally, the best place to see the warrior gardens is the small town of Chiran in the south of Kyushu, where a whole street of lovely Samurai gardens has been preserved. The two gardening styles began a common development from a certain moment on, as the Samurai were followers of Zen Buddhism, which arrived in Japan in the 12th century. The rigid disciplinarian rules of Zen and its meditative search for truth suited the philosophy of the warriors. Many Samurais who were kept frantically busy in the 15th and 16th century – due to the permanent unrests – obtained a lot of strength and tranquility from calligraphy, painting and the art of gardening. According to the Zen philosophy, the Chinese landscape paintings captured the ideal beauty. So Zen masters created craggy cliff formations, dry waterfalls and riverbeds and moss-covered coasts alongside small oceans – out of immaculately raked pebbles.

As so often in this country, expectations and reality, theory and practical experience diverge widely. Only very few Japanese can enjoy the inspiring view over their own lovely garden. The average lots are far too small, and if there is the choice between a landscaped garden and a car park, no one will hesitate to choose a car park. (Particularly as no car license is issued without proof of a car park.)

Most people living in Tokyo relax in the public parks, such as the huge and lovely Shinjuku Gyoen. It was created on the property of a feudal lord (this tells you a lot about the feudal lords of ancient Japan and how they liked to live) and originally only the emperor was allowed to access it. Here he could not only admire the Japanese art of gardening, but could also be amazed by examples of the English and French culture of gardening. It was only after World War II – when the tenno had to give up his godliness, a few other privileges and the exclusive right to access this beautiful park – that the Shinjuku Gyoen was opened to the public.

But for determined flower-lovers there are other ways out of the lack of space and the lack of gardens. They have found ways of creating their own little green and blooming oases, despite the tightness of Japan's cities. In front of many house entries, particularly of old houses which show their age, often half the street is occupied and entrances are framed person-high by lovely, sprawling, chaotic gardens of potted plants. The owners of these potted plants are not trying to create little works of art in a proper style, they just enjoy a bit of green, even if it's often in the way. Occasion-

1 The temple garden of Sanzen-in. **2** A treasure deep in the province – one of the Samurai gardens of Chiran, Kyushu. **3** The main attraction of Kyoto – the Golden Pavilion, which is completely overcrowded in fall.

Miniature universe: the garden of Ryoanji

Each morning at 5 a.m. young monks rake away the leaves and twigs from the ground in Ryoanji Temple Garden in Kyoto. The mastermind of this landscape, about the size of half a tennis court, was the landscape architect Soami (1455–1525). It is Japan's most famous and most frequently visited example of *karesansui* – the dry landscape. It truly is a small universe, a perfect image of peace and contemplation, a playing field for the spirit. A place where it can roam freely.

But during the opening hours there won't be much time for that. The tourist sitting on the wooden steps of the temple,

seeking tranquility, will look down on a perfectly raked, gray sea of pebbles from which a few rocky islands, covered in moss, emerge. To you and me, who aren't in the know, the reddish wall which surrounds the garden looks as though it could do with a lick of paint. But precisely that is its secret. This wall has grown and developed the way it is now. Its weathered surface is particular evidence of its sublime being. Usually the many tourists (foreigners as well as Japanese who find this exercise a little strange, too) stand here without moving for an average of five minutes in the hope of some sort of enlightenment. But they are sorely disappointed to find that they could sit here for five hours or even five days without having made any progress at all. This, strictly speaking, is an important Zen experience.

ally these little gardens make you stop in your tracks and realize how little you need in order to create something amazing. In countries such as Germany this lack of order would probably attract the attention of the police. Here the people are left alone as everyone benefits from their passion. These people, the urban flower-lovers, are the actual heroes of the Japanese art of gardening.

Immerse Yourself and Feel Good
The culture of bathing – Japan's greatest passion

With its 27,000 hot springs, Japan has been the bathing paradise since ancient times. Its numerous volcanoes and subterranean fires are responsible for this wealth of bubbling, warm water. The Japanese bathing culture cannot be compared in the least to our bathing culture where the weekly bath was considered the peak of cleanliness – up until well into the 20th century.

In 1904, Basil Hall Chamberlain, the veteran of research on Japan, noted: "Cleanliness is one of the few truly indigenous phenomena of the Japanese civilization. Many other things originated in China, not so the bath tub. Even in the lower classes, people constantly wash and scrub themselves – a Japanese crowd smells better than any other crowd world-wide."

But the Japanese are not only driven into hot water to smell good and to be clean. The daily bath also supports the balance of their souls and bodies, the harmony.

"The European bathing culture is a culture of rinsing," bathing professor Matsuda Tadanori of the University of Sapporo explained to me. "The Japanese bathing culture on the other hand is a culture of immersion, of soaking. We literally sink our bodies up to our necks into the hot water. This is how we cleanse our heart from worries and tension. In the bath we regenerate our energy, our strength.

Even Japan's myths are full of bathing scenes. And to this day you can hear Japanese sigh: "Ahhh, gokuraku – the (Buddhist) paradise" while they lower themselves into the hot water. Maybe the oldest public thermal bath in the country is the Dogo-Onsen in Matsuyama on Shikoku. They say that even the antique emperors used to come here to relax and heal their ailments.

The traveling foreigner will notice that even in the business hotels which aren't very charming, but good value, the bathrooms are watertight (and often disconcertingly wobbly) cells made of cream-colored plastic and the bathtubs are rather short, but deep. The manufacturers simply assume that – as the Japanese bathing etiquette dictates – the hotel guest will have a proper shower and scrub before he climbs into the bath to relax (!) and not to cleanse himself (!).

1 The first wellness centers in the world – Japan's public baths. 2 Energy conservation: boiling eggs in the "hells" of Beppu. 3 The relaxation bath isn't quite as hot. It should ideally be a pleasant 42 degrees centigrade. 4 The Japanese love their baths and waterfalls.

1 Well run onsen are cleaned daily. 2 If there's not enough time – a hot foot bath at least. 3 The ideal ofuro – natural rock and view over the landscape. 4 Bathing beauties never go out of fashion on Japanese TV.

But even in Japan, hot water does not equal hot water. A bath at home in Tokyo or Osaka, filled with hot water from the boiler, will not give nearly the same pleasure as a hot bath in Beppu, Kusatsu or Kinosaki, just to mention a few of the well-known baths – or *onsen* as they are called. *Onsen* is a magic word for the Japanese. As soon as they hear it they visualize warm, wafting clouds of steam, steamed-up mirrors and ideally a view over a snowy valley, mountains with dense forests, a river or a rocky coastal landscape. And afterwards: a delicious meal.

Onsen means natural spring. According to the *Onsen* law from 1948, a spring can only be called *onsen* if the water gushing from its rocks is at least 25 degrees centigrade and contains a certain amount of minerals. The word *onsen* is similar, but only *similar*, to the German word "Bad", which is stuck onto town names to signify

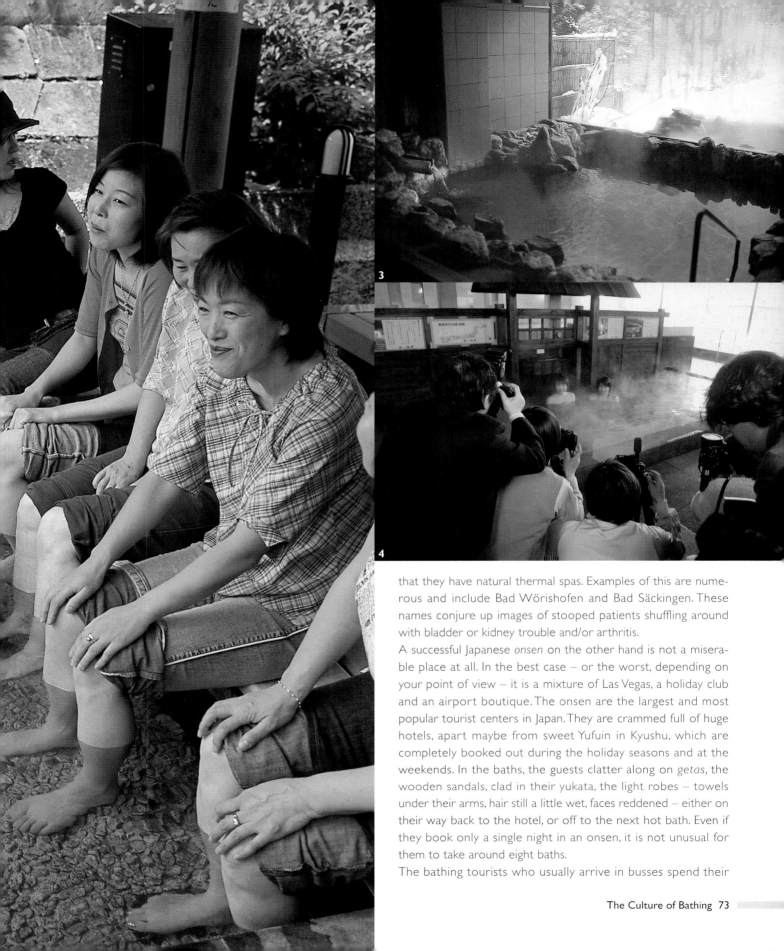

that they have natural thermal spas. Examples of this are numerous and include Bad Wörishofen and Bad Säckingen. These names conjure up images of stooped patients shuffling around with bladder or kidney trouble and/or arthritis.

A successful Japanese *onsen* on the other hand is not a miserable place at all. In the best case – or the worst, depending on your point of view – it is a mixture of Las Vegas, a holiday club and an airport boutique. The onsen are the largest and most popular tourist centers in Japan. They are crammed full of huge hotels, apart maybe from sweet Yufuin in Kyushu, which are completely booked out during the holiday seasons and at the weekends. In the baths, the guests clatter along on *getas*, the wooden sandals, clad in their yukata, the light robes – towels under their arms, hair still a little wet, faces reddened – either on their way back to the hotel, or off to the next hot bath. Even if they book only a single night in an onsen, it is not unusual for them to take around eight baths.

The bathing tourists who usually arrive in busses spend their

weekends in the *onsen*. They stay at the *ryokan*, the traditional inns which serve gorgeous food. The Japanese even see *onsen* on TV – several times a day. The popular travel programs consist to an amazingly large extent of pictures of young women lowering themselves into the hot water crying: *"Kimochi!* – what a lovely feeling!" Of course they aren't naked, but are modestly wrapped in towels. Contrary to the distorted idea, which is widespread in the west, the Japanese baths have nothing, absolutely nothing to do with sexuality. The Japanese baths are as free of sex as, say, the corridors of a local government office. If the Japanese connect sex with hot water at all, they call it "Turkish bath" – a result of their own distorted ideas of what goes on in other parts of the world. Nudity in the baths is completely normal in Japan. Even old Chamberlain reported: "They see it, but don't notice it." Mixed baths were widespread, particularly in the countryside. Only Western ideas of moral and the worries of

1 The oldest bath in the country – the Dogo-Onsen in Matsuyama, Shikoku. 2 Modern baths at Lake Toya in Hokkaido. 3 Bathing guests clad in their yukata in Kinosaki-onsen. 4 The character "Yu" on the curtain promises hot water. 5 Beppu in Kyushu has the most hot springs in the country. 6 Close by – idyllic Yufuin.

Japanese politicians about general modesty brought about the separation of males and females.

Ideally the *ofuro*, the Japanese bath that you'll find in good hotels and *ryokan*, is divided into an inner part with a wooden tub, ideally made of cedar wood hundreds of years old, and an exterior part, the *roten*. Ideally the roten is surrounded by natural rock with a view over a magnificent landscape. Again ideally they are cleaned and scrubbed daily, as a slippery film very quickly covers all surfaces due to the minerals in the water.

But the baths aren't always small. Especially the popular entertainment centers have huge areas the size of gyms to cater for their hundreds of visitors. There are dozens of pools of various sizes, of various temperatures (although the most common temperature is 42 degrees centigrade) and various styles – some of which get taking used to. But the rows of low showers are always the same. The bathers sit under the showerheads on low stools, washing themselves with soap and hot water, which they pour over themselves from small wooden tubs. It is considered bad style to stand up during this procedure, as the foreigners, who are used to standing up in their showers, occasionally do. In general, foreigners still cause amazement and occasionally even cause panic. The Japanese don't trust us quite enough to voluntarily share their bathwater with us. This led to all sorts of ugly incidences in the little port town of Otaru in Hokkaido. *"Japanese only"* signs, which were considered racist, were put up in front of several of the baths. The Russian seamen, of which there are a lot in this region, were known for rudely ignoring the Japanese

bathing etiquette. But even the well-educated and *onsen*-experienced foreign guest will sometimes receive skeptical looks and the showers next to him will usually remain unused. And when he lowers himself into the communal bath, his Japanese bathing pals may sometimes leave it in a panic.

During my first stay in Japan in 1986 nobody in the *sento* was courageous enough to sit at a spot which could theoretically be contaminated by the water running down from my spot. The *sento*, which can be translated as the "penny bath", is the traditional public bath. Ideally there is one in every neighborhood, instantly recognizable by its high chimney. Far into the 20th century the *sento* was the center of every Japanese community. This

is where the neighborhood met for a chat, for jolly scrubbing and shampooing.

The *sento* was a place of relaxation and recuperation and a place where children learned about life. The arrival of affordable bathroom technology and the triumphant revolution of the shower gradually led to the demise of this traditional public bath. In 1965 there were 2,641 *sento* in Tokyo. Now less than half of them are left – a total of 1,160 remain.

I A strong will is needed on the way to spiritual purity – the icy cold bath. **2** Men and women usually have separate baths, but there are exceptions. **3** The hot sand bath in Ibusuki, south Kyushu, eases rheumatism and stress.

Misogi – Cult of cold water

It is a fundamental belief of the Japanese that water has purifying properties – not only physically, but also spiritually. In front of every Shinto shrine you'll find a bubbling spring where visitors should wash their hands and rinse out their mouths to alleviate themselves of their worldly impurities. The cleansing procedure, the so called *misogi*, is mentioned in the oldest Japanese record, the Kojiki, which was written in 712. According to the Kojiki, it all started with the deities Izanagi and Izanami who created Japan according to the legends. The ascetic variation of the cleansing procedure is to stand under an icy cold waterfall.

The gentlemen in the photograph to the left were taking part in a *misogi* ritual in Ise, at the highest shrine of the Shinto religion. The whole thing was organized by the Japanese Chamber of Industry and Commerce. The wintry bath in the river, an icy four degrees centigrade, is the highlight of each of these weekend workshops. It is supposed to increase their sensitivity towards the needs and wishes of their colleagues and their self-awareness, an understanding of their own strengths and weaknesses.

Lessons in Japanese Hospitality
A visit to the ryokan

If you've taken the long flight to Japan upon yourself and you're curious to find out more about this unknown country, you've earned a special treat. It is different from a night in the luxury hotels which are always the same and certainly better than a night in the depressing business hotels with their minuscule rooms and the swaying bath cells, let alone in the notorious capsule hotels. A night in a traditional Japanese inn, the *ryokan*, will be expensive, but it will be an experience that you'll never forget. Let's pay a visit to the "Tawaraya" in Kyoto, as it is considered the best ryokan in the country. Let's imagine that the price of up to 600 euros a night per person won't make us faint immediately. Many famous people have stayed here, including Karl Gustav and Sylvia of Sweden, Marlon Brando, Barbra Streisand and Jean-Paul Sartre.

We arrive at a well-kept façade in a side street of Kyoto. It looks nice, but doesn't hint at anything too luxurious. Through the wooden door we enter a quiet little courtyard. We take off our shoes before entering the building. There's a polite shoe guy who takes your shoes, bowing several times. When you are about to leave, he will have them ready for you. A young woman kneels in front of us, bowing so deeply that her forehead almost touches the tatami *mats on the floor. She welcomes us with an enthusiastic "Irasshaimasse!"* Then she grabs our suitcase, which weighs about two tons, and carries it effortlessly across the wooden floors into our room. We notice antiques which have been placed around the room nicely and lovely flower arrangements. There is nothing overwhelming or showy. Nothing screaming out at you: "Watch it, I cost 30,000 euros!" Nothing to completely absorb our attention or intimidate us. The connoisseur amongst us will recognize that some of the pieces of furniture and art could well be shown in a museum. But it doesn't matter either way. We are supposed to feel comfortable here. The room rep – this is what the chambermaids are called in the "Tawaraya" – leads us to one of the 18 rooms, which has a name – such as "Bamboo" or "Fuji" or "Wealth" – instead of a number. She motions us to sit down at the low table and disappears again to serve us the ritual welcome tea. Our eye wanders out

1 The boundary between the room and the garden is blurred. **2** The bundle of brushwood is the sign of the "Tawaraya". **3** The garden becomes part of your living room. **4** The entry to this inn is a homage to the seasons.

into an incredibly perfect garden, a landscape of green moss, ferns and stone lanterns, a water trough and low trees. This is the moment where we forget that we are right in the middle of a large city, in the 21st century. It is a magic garden which is ours for this one night. We are supposed to enjoy the view of it whole-heartedly. The room is divided into two. The floor of one half is covered by *tatami* mats, the traditional floor covering, the other with wooden parquet. Antique furniture, precious vases and beautiful tapestries create a special ambience. Each piece has a story to tell, elegantly carrying its age of many hundreds of years with dignity. Everything has the air of history and the sublime. A knowledgeable guest will recognize that this is a calligraphy of a revered monk of the 17th century and that is an invaluable piece of pottery from the workshops of Kiyomizu.

Set into the wall is the *tokonoma*, the attractive alcove of every tra-ditional Japanese reception room. It is sparingly decorated with a script roll or a picture roll and a vase – quite probably from the 13th century – containing an ikebana arrangement. The place in front of the *tokonoma* is the place of honor in Japan. The guest who is the highest in the hierarchical order sits here, with his back to the tokonoma. He cannot see the little shrine of art, but becomes part of it.

Kyoto is not known for its hot springs, so the "Tawaraya" isn't an *onsen-ryokan*. But the bath is duly celebrated here, too: every room has its own, exclusive tub.

1 Select antiques and works of art are placed unobtrusively in the corners of the rooms. **2** The tokonoma – the heart of the Japanese reception room. **3** Inconspicuous, but dignified – the front of the "Tawaraya". **4** All rooms lead into the garden.

The room rep returns with our tea, bowing again very deeply, introducing herself, welcoming us warmly again and making conversation with us while she serves us the tea and a bite to eat. Assuming we aren't Japanologists, we don't understand a word. This makes her giggle, and maybe she can speak a few words of English. If she can't, she'll appear with a dictionary next time she comes to our service. She is determined to make every sacrifice and do everything in her power, as she is responsible for making us feel comfortable. It is her responsibility to make our stay pleasurable and relaxing. Before leaving, she asks us when we would deign to have dinner. At 7:30 p.m. That's very late for a ryokan. Japanese guests often want to have dinner at 6:00 p.m., so that they have more time to spend in the bath.

The Japanese *ryokan* is not cheap, but the price does include two meals. And these aren't any old meals, it is the best food that Japan's cuisine can offer! The room rep will disappear and reappear again just before dinner time to serve us our food in our

1 After dinner the chambermaid sets up the futon. **2** You don't notice the other guests. **3** Simple elegance, noble understatement – the trademark of this ryokan.

room. She brings everything in separately, bowl for bowl, course for course. She will head for the kitchen around 15 times to bring us all the delightful delicacies which are arranged in bowls, on little plates, pottery and lacquer work which an expert will recognize as magnificent works of art. Each bite to eat and every course has its own receptacle with its own special design and its own history. The various types of plates, bowls and saucers are as diverse as Japan's cuisine itself. The Japanese concept of a successful meal is "to enjoy the meal and the way it is served". The rice is served at the end, like in China. It is supposed to satiate the person who might still feel a little hungry after having enjoyed all the other tasty morsels. Although we did receive a calligraphically artistic menu at the onset of the meal, we couldn't read it. To console you: even if we could read part of it, we still wouldn't have been able to understand a lot of it, even if we had spent five years of our lives studying Japanese. At university they simply forget to teach students of Japanese important concepts such as "lightly roasted sea cucumber ovaries". So the room rep will try to explain the delicacies with which the chef is spoiling us today, and she will also assist us, where necessary, to use the sauces and dips in the correct manner.

After dinner we leave the table and retreat into the next room, go for a walk, dip into the hot bath, in any case render ourselves invisible so that the room rep can prepare our bed in peace. It is a futon which is stowed away in a deep wardrobe behind the sliding doors during the day. After she's done that, she will leave our room, shuffling her feet while she walks. This is polite behavior – in the Japanese houses, which are not exactly sound-proof, you announce your coming and going by shuffling. Before she finally leaves us for the night, she asks what time we would like to have breakfast. Maybe at 8 a.m.? A night in a *ryokan* is not

suited to those who like to lie in. Usually you need to clear your room between 10 a.m. and 11 a.m.

Next morning the room rep will reappear to store the futon back in its wardrobe and to serve us the most incredible breakfast imaginable: fried fish with slivers of ginger, steamed tofu and *yuba*, tofu cream and mushrooms, rice with dried seaweed, and a poached egg in soy sauce. Maybe on the side tiny dried fishes, delicious with soy sauce and rice, pickled gherkins, turnips and spinach rolls, *miso* (soy paste) soup and tea. And when we leave the ryokan, both the room rep and the receptionist will stand at the door and watch us leave in our taxi and they won't move until we have disappeared around the corner. And as there is a set of red lights in front of the "Tawaraya", this procedure can take several minutes. Finally they will both bow again deeply.

Not every *ryokan* has the same works of art and the same uplifting view over the gardens. The "Tawaraya" is famous for that. And not every *ryokan* is as expensive. And you don't always enter a building which is 150 years old. Some, especially the *ryokan* in the popular *onsen*, are nothing more than enormous hotels, not particularly attractive from the outside. But still, a good ryokan will offer service similar to that at the "Tawaraya": the warm welcome, the meals in the room, the futons to sleep on, the shuffling, discreet room reps. And the food, these refined compositions of delicacies, possibly the best food in Japan. For me it is the best food in the world!

The pinnacle of hospitality

If you stay in the "Tawaraya" at the weekend, you may have the chance to experience a tea ceremony. This is one of the greatest mysteries of Japanese hospitality and is certainly also one of the most tiring things for your legs, as you sit on them the whole time. The tea ceremony is a cult exercise in refinement, humility and politeness in this country of stylized rules, rituals and perfectly choreographed details. I fear that only very few foreigners have ever managed to grasp it properly, to really enjoy it, whilst still being able to behave properly in the way that is expected.

Nothing that happens in the tiny room, which you enter through a door only 90 centimeters high, forcing even the proudest guest to bow, is left to chance. Nothing is haphazard. Everything is deliberate. This includes the sparse, but select, decoration which the host has arranged for this one day only, for these particular guests, to celebrate the irretrievability of the moment. This includes the selection of the accessories: the pot of water, the little wooden tea spoons, the tea whisk and the tea bowls. These utensils can be hundreds of years old and the guest is expected to show his respect and admiration for them. By the way, an antique tea whisk from an old tea master can cost up to 100,000 euros. The food and sweets that are served with the tea are delicious and dissolve the bitterness of the strong, bright green tea in a magical way, creating a truly uplifting experience for your taste buds.

1 Peak activity in the kitchen – each dish is brought to your room.
2 At first it seems strange, later you can't do without it: breakfast with rice and marinated vegetables, miso soup, tofu and fried fish. The picture shows the breakfast at the "Tawaraya".

A Whole Lot of Fish
The auction of Japan's favorite food

Before we return to the amazing and soulful works of art of Japanese haute cuisine, I recommend a little trip to the place where all these things are bought – the sea cucumber ovaries, the bits of bass, the tidbits made from tuna belly and the strips of seaweed. Let's have a look at Tsukiji fish market in Tokyo. Watch out! We were almost run over by one of these kamikaze pilots who race around the market with their fast little motor trolleys, a cigarette dangling from the corner of their mouth, as though they own the place. A morning visit to Tsukiji is certainly nothing for weak nerves. At first Tsukiji doesn't sound like a place worth seeing. The main bout of activity happens before 6 a.m., an unearthly hour. And it revolves only around dead fish. How can that be educational and exciting? But it is! The tuna auction at this fish market is a "must" during your visit to Tokyo.

First you have to find your way through a large labyrinth, around 22 hectares large. This is where the almost 1,000 wholesalers and agents barricade themselves behind pools, basins, buckets and polystyrene boxes. (A total of 15,000 people work at Tsukiji fish market and the neighboring fruit and vegetable wholesale market.) This market supplies the entire Kanto plain, the supermarkets, the fish stores and the restaurants – over 30 million hungry customers – with their favorite food, every day except for Sunday. The diversity at this market – the largest fish market in the world, with a daily turnover of 2,300 tons – is almost endless. You'll discover many weird and sometimes scary-looking creatures in the basins and buckets, on ice or sealed in plastic. I hadn't any idea which weird things live on this planet, let alone that they are edible. But they all have a firm place on the Japanese menu. Since ancient times the Japanese have always experimented with any seafood they could find, trying different ways of preparing it, to see if it can be made palatable. There is no other nation in the world that eats more fish than the Japanese. You'll find the best ambience in the tuna halls, shortly before the hectic auction starts. With an ecstatic look on their faces the experts rub the icy meat of the deep-frozen fish between their fingers to assess its fat content. The fattier the meat, the better

1 Secret signs and funny songs – the tuna auction in Tsukiji. 2 Frozen giants – the deep-frozen goods. 3 The best pieces are displayed like jewels in a showcase. 4 The fresh tuna is flown in daily from all around the world.

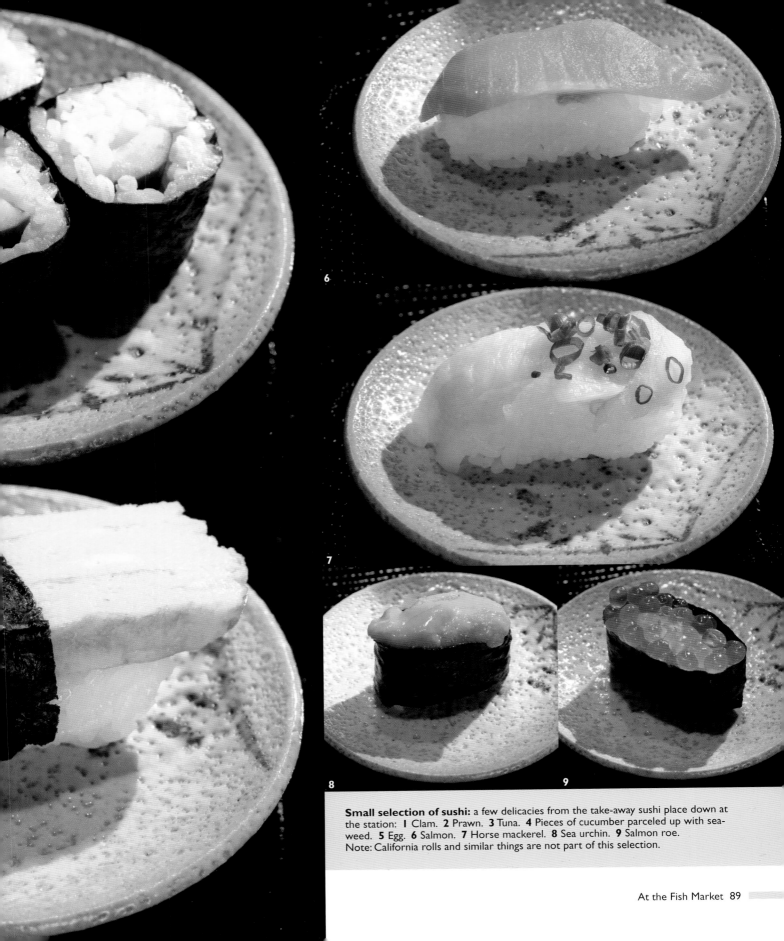

Small selection of sushi: a few delicacies from the take-away sushi place down at the station: **1** Clam. **2** Prawn. **3** Tuna. **4** Pieces of cucumber parceled up with seaweed. **5** Egg. **6** Salmon. **7** Horse mackerel. **8** Sea urchin. **9** Salmon roe.
Note: California rolls and similar things are not part of this selection.

its taste. They walk along the rows of stiff fish which are enveloped by a fog of thawing ice, clutching their grapnels, choosing those objects for which they want to bid. An awful lot of money is involved. The trust of their regular customers, which has developed over the years, weighs on them. In this country of fish gourmets, every dealer has a reputation to defend. The fresh tuna are laid out in the great hall. The wholesalers cast their professional eyes mainly at their bellies. The fatty, pink belly flesh – referred to as toro – is cut into filets for the much-loved sushi. The highest price that has been bid for this part of the tuna was around 1,000 euros per kilogram.

If you can decipher the little yellow signs showing where these fish came from, you'll feel as though you're at an international conference for dead tuna. They come from South Africa, Fiji, Chile, the Maldives, Spain, Turkey and Taiwan. The Japanese search the world's oceans for the best fish. Then they make sure that it is killed properly, put on ice and loaded onto the next airplane to Tokyo: luxury fish for the gourmets.

1 Loading up the loot of the day. **2** Barrows are one mode of transport… **3** …but the motor trolleys are faster. **4** The expensive fish has to be cut extremely carefully. **5** They will be served as sushi and sashimi today.

Sushi master Suzuki – a wizard of sushi

Mister Suzuki Tsugio is one of the thousands of sushi cooks who go to Tsukiji market every morning to buy what they need for the day. He has a little sushi restaurant, where a maximum of ten people can sit at the counter watching him prepare their food. They are mainly regulars who trust his opinion and knowledge. As is usual in the good sushi restaurants, there is no menu. You sit down and ask: "What would you recommend today?" and he gets going immediately. Mister Suzuki has been in this profession for sixteen years and is the purest professor of sushi, like every experienced and committed sushi master in this country. He knows everything about any

fish that is known to humankind. He knows how best to make it taste delicious. This one tastes best roasted lightly. That one, such as the young Allis shad, should be salted first and left to marinate. He knows that summer is the best season for abalone and that the best horse mackerel is caught from around Awajishima in the Inland Sea. And he also knows about the historical specialties of his trade. For instance, the cooks in Osaka, the old merchant and trade center, slit the eel's belly, which makes sense with regard to their eel-like shape. But the cooks in Tokyo haven't got the heart to do that. Tokyo was heavily influenced by the Samurai, and the Kyoto way of cutting eels reminds them too much of the ritualistic suicide of the samurai, the *seppuku*. We know this fatal act as hara-kiri, the courageous thrust of the sword through the belly.

Mister Suzuki also knows that you can only filet the fish known as kocho with the so-called daimyoo-zoroshi, the feudal cut, because of its tough, crooked bones. It is called "feudal", because it leaves a luxurious amount of flesh remaining on the bones. (Regarding the kocho, I am sorry but even my trusted dictionary – which has hardly ever let me down at any restaurant – doesn't know what this fish might be. It tells me that a kocho is a migratory bird. But even I know that that's wrong. We're talking about a fish, not a bird.) Mister Suzuki also knows that the sole is better in summer and that the halibut is best in fall and winter and that the fins and the bones are great for making soups and so on.

I really don't want to spoil your appetite, but what these smart restaurants serve up and what you can now buy as a snack which remains fresh for three days, sealed in a plastic pack– trust me, whatever it is, it is not sushi…

Aesthetically Pleasing
The delights of the Japanese cuisine

The most important word of the Japanese cuisine isn't sushi, as you might expect, but shun. This word describes the season in which this or that vegetable, fruit or sea creature tastes best. We are familiar with this concept to some extent. We've got the "asparagus season" or the "mussel season". But our cuisine isn't nearly as diverse, traditional and pure and not nearly as closely linked to the different seasons as the Japanese cuisine. Almost every dish of the Japanese haute cuisine is tied to a particular month. It represents a bow to nature and a celebration of it.

Bamboo sprouts are eaten in spring, after the cherry trees have blossomed. You enjoy the big, white *Daikon* beets in winter. November is the month for the notorious puffer fish and the crabs from the Sea of Japan. You'll only find the flowers of the rape plant and the leaves of the chrysanthemum for your soup in spring. The first catch of the *sanman*, the Pacific Saury, in the fishing community of Kessennuma in North Japan is a national autumnal event. The eel was praised as the perfect food in the oppressive summer heat as early as the eighth century. And late October is the best time for *matsutake* mushrooms.

Fish and seafood always formed the basis of the Japanese cuisine. This isn't surprising for a nation which lies in the middle of the sea and is surrounded by the richest fishing grounds in the world. From the sixth century on, since Buddhism spread in Japan, meat and animal fats were almost taboo, at least in public. But the Japanese seemed to have made fish an exception. However, despite the glorious history of a highly developed meatless monastic cuisine, to this day vegetarians have a hard time in Japan. If you say, "Please, no meat!" you'll most likely get the following response: "What – not even fish? Or at least chicken?"

The Japanese cuisine reaches total perfection in the *kaiseki* (haute cuisine) which you'll find in expensive restaurants and the traditional inns, the *ryokan*.

None of the delicious dishes which form part of a full-blown *kaiseki* meal have a very strong taste of their own. The standard spices are quite mild: for instance soy sauce, cooking wine *(mirin)*, soy paste *(miso)* and vinegar. Additional flavor is provided by herbs and roots: green horseradish *(wasabi)*, ginger, perilla and yellow-wood. It

1 Seasonal fruit and leaves are used for decoration. **2** This makes eating fun – countless little bowls, saucers and plates. **3** The guest grills the beef and vegetables on his own table grill. **4** Tasty, varied and healthy – the traditional breakfast.

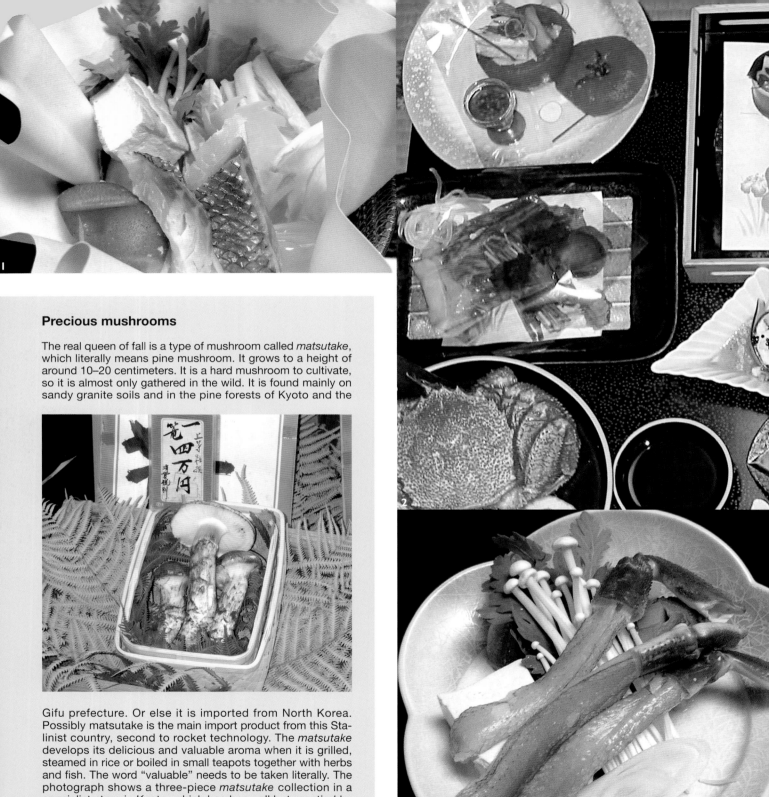

Precious mushrooms

The real queen of fall is a type of mushroom called *matsutake*, which literally means pine mushroom. It grows to a height of around 10–20 centimeters. It is a hard mushroom to cultivate, so it is almost only gathered in the wild. It is found mainly on sandy granite soils and in the pine forests of Kyoto and the

Gifu prefecture. Or else it is imported from North Korea. Possibly matsutake is the main import product from this Stalinist country, second to rocket technology. The *matsutake* develops its delicious and valuable aroma when it is grilled, steamed in rice or boiled in small teapots together with herbs and fish. The word "valuable" needs to be taken literally. The photograph shows a three-piece *matsutake* collection in a specialist store in Kyoto, which has been all but emptied by avid mushroom gourmets. The price label for these three mushrooms reads 40,000 yen. Just for fun, try to convert this into euros yourself. You'll get a feel for how valued these mushrooms are.

is the combination of the various ingredients, spices and dishes which makes up the perfectly choreographed complete culinary pleasure.

The Japanese cook doesn't believe in lengthy cooking times. The presentation of the food, the experience of having it beautifully served, the synchronization of colors, the order and the fine allusions to the seasons is much more important. The aesthetic balance of forms, sizes and structures, the harmony between appearance and taste represents the main focus. This is why you will never sit down at a completely laid table for your meals. Each bite to eat, each course will be served separately on a different plate, on a different dish or saucer. A high-class Japanese meal does not have a main course. There are many little highlights, something raw and something fried, a soup, something steamed and then a stew which is cooked up at the table and maybe something deep-fried. The aim is not to feel full at the end of such a meal, the aim is to feel content.

1 Fish, tofu and vegetables are braised at the table in fire-proof paper.
2 Each sauce, each dish, each garnish is served on a special plate. 3 Steamed, grilled or raw – and always accompanied by a delicious sauce. 4 A feast for the eye: Japan's top cooks have a refined senses of aesthetics.

Expensive beef

Beef is a relatively new addition to the Japanese menu and only conquered the nation's palates in a big way with the *meiji* restoration after 1868. Of course the beef was adapted to the Japanese rules and the Japanese taste, like everything that arrived from abroad. Good and expensive beef has a lot of fat

and is usually cooked in winter. Mainly in winter the Japanese make rich soups out of it and add vegetables and glass noodles. These pots of bubbling broth are known as *sukiyaki* and *shabushabu*. The centers of meat production are Matsuzaka, Kobe, Omi and recently also Hida. Here the cattle is fattened up, groomed and massaged, kept in good spirits with nutritious cocktails of grain and an occasional sip of beer in the hot summer. When the time comes to auction the animals off, they look like tons on legs. In the supermarket you'll pay 3,000 yen for 300 grams of Hida beef to make your *sukiyaki*. That's around 22 euros. The beef from Matsuzaka is even more expensive.

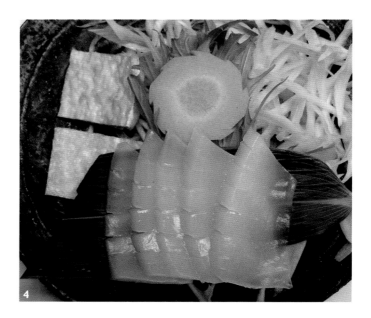

In the Land of Delicious Snacks
Fast food beyond the hot dog

Please bear with me if I dive yet a little deeper into the topic of Japanese food. Admittedly it is one of my favorite topics. But on top of that many foreigners are easily intimidated by the occasionally strange, but always delicious – or at least healthy – dishes of this country. Consequently they simply miss out on some of the most incredible pleasures.

It is almost as though Japan were facing a constant threat of a famine. There is such a large variety of snack bars and little diners which make our hot dog stalls look positively poor. I know you'll keep on hearing that Japan and Tokyo are so terribly expensive so that you can hardly afford to eat. I assure you that you won't need to pay more than ten euros at any of the many snack bars.

The Japanese version of our sandwich is called *onigiri*. This is a triangular seaweed wrap of rice mixed with things like sour marinated plums, salmon or tuna mayonnaise.

Apart from the little skewers that you get, onigiri and curry rice are the only two snacks which are not usually eaten using chopsticks, but with a spoon (in the case of the curry rice) or just as they are (in the case of the *onigiri*). If you find it hard to handle chopsticks, there is no need to feel embarrassed. On the contrary. Obviously most Japanese still assume that we are simply helpless without knife and fork. If we, the *gaijin* (foreigners), manage to eat our food the way they do, they often react with exaggerated admiration.

What French fries are to us, noodles are to the Japanese. They particularly like *soba* – dark buckwheat noodles which are usually served in a spicy broth. A variety of things are added, such as deep-fried prawns or green vegetables. This kind of soup can also contain thick, white, rather slithery noodles. This kind of noodle is called *udon*. Watch out – for beginners, they are tricky to manage with chopsticks. In summer the *soba* are often served cold, accompanied by a spicy brew containing chives and *wasabi* (the hot, green horseradish paste which is also served with sushi and *sashimi* and which a few scientists believe contains nuclear fuels). When served cold, the dark noodles are called *zarusoba*. I could tell you a very embarrassing story of what happened when I first ordered *zarusoba* many years ago. I was full of virtue, an enthusiastic student

1 *Onigiri* is the name of the Japanese version of our sandwich – rice balls wrapped in seaweed. **2** If the noren curtain is hanging outside, then the restaurant is open. **3** Yakitori – chicken skewers. **4** A classic of the rural cook shops: grilled dwarf salmon in salt crust.

Okashi are little snacks and biscuits of significant cultural importance. Every tourist destination in Japan has a huge variety of them and any traveler is required by law to buy a pack of *okashi* or other local specialties for his loved ones at home. My recommendations are: **1** *Udon* noodles. **2** Roots in a spicy marinade. **3** Sour marinated beets. **4** Beans and dried fish. **5** *Senbei* rice crackers. **6** Biscuits made of soy paste or of fermented soy beans. **7** Cabbage for the soup.

and ordered this dish in fluent high Japanese. But luckily we haven't got time for that! Please just remember that the brew I mentioned above is a dip (!) and not a cold soup (!). You dip your noodles into it, rather than eating the noodles first and then occasionally taking a sip of what you think is a soup…

Another little survival tip: most modern soba bars don't accept cash, they expect you to pull a ticket at their machine. A prerequisite for being able to do this though is at least a rudimentary knowledge of the Japanese letters or else a sense of adventure and culinary flexibility.

Another fundamental Japanese noodle experience are the *raamen*. These white, slightly curly noodles also swim in a lovely, rich soup, accompanied by bamboo sprouts, soy seedlings, boiled egg and slices of roast pork.

These noodle soups are not simply eaten, they are sucked in or, better said, inhaled with loud slurping noises. Experts swear that

the pleasure of eating is increased by proper slurping. We *gaijin* will probably never really understand this mystery, as we are terrible slurpers. Either we sip much too gingerly, looking around again and again to check whether we aren't making a bad impression, or else we finally throw all deeply ingrained inhibitions about slurping overboard and are so loud that even the Japanese look over to see what the source of all this noise is.

I am sure that you're aware that sushi can also be consumed as fast food on a conveyor belt. You will find this all over the world and I am sure that such a place has opened near you. (And I shall hold back the remark that even the Japanese fast food sushi is far superior to any average European or American restaurant sushi.)

Whilst the tasty noodle soups are usually served in buildings, along counters, the soba is also served at 24-hour bars where you stand while you eat. These bars are often found at gas stations or at train stations. You'll find the widest spectrum of traditional fast food at

1 Conveyer-belt sushi. You pay according to the number and color of the plates. 2 *Oden* – steamed food – for instance, lotus roots, beets or tofu. 3 The bits of chicken have to be grilled on charcoal. 4 *Soba* – buckwheat noodles in a spicy broth, often with herbs, fish pie and battered herring. 5 *Okonomi-yaki,* pancakes smothered with cabbage, ginger and egg.

the colorful street stalls and booths. Lots of them are set up at every event, including the matsuri and the shrine festivals. They line the large gardens and parks during the cherry blossom season and feed the guests at festivals and rock concerts. The most important word that you should learn here is yaki – it refers to anything fried.

The pride of every store

Every Japanese restaurant, even good noodle counters and many stores, especially the old ones, hang the so-called *noren* above their entries. They may best be described as shop curtains with slits. They used to be predominantly blue with white writing. Now they come in any color you can imagine. The name of the establishment and its coat of arms – if it has one – is printed on or weaved into them. Japanese houses had these curtains as early as the eighth century to keep the sand and dust outside. Nowadays they mainly signify:

Welcome, we are open. Noren aren't simply curtains, they express the pride and identity of the shop owner. My dictionary defines an old, traditional shop as *"Noren-no furui mise"* – meaning a shop with an old *noren*. The noren force the customer or guest who is entering the place to bow symbolically. I don't know whether this is deliberate or not, but it is appropriate in any case and contributes to a harmonious atmosphere.

On hotplates and grills you'll find *yakitori* – chicken skewers with leek; takoyaki – pastry balls with squid; *okonomiyaki* – pancakes with cabbage, ginger and egg; *yakisoba* – fried noodles with cabbage and ginger, without egg. Next door they may have prepared beef skewers, bananas coated in chocolate and sausage skewers (they are called *"Furankufuruto"* in Japanese – just like the German city which the Japanese probably imagine as a kind of sausage paradise) and steamed potatoes. If you're lucky you might even come across *sakana-shioyaki* – skewers of salted and grilled fish.

All of this is served on plastic or styrofoam dishes, and you are provided with disposable chopsticks. This isn't only dubious in terms of a waste of resources. After you've eaten, you will often be faced with the serious problem of how to dispose of your tools, as the Japanese don't think much of public garbage cans. So you'll probably simply look around to see where other people have dumped their used things and lay yours next to theirs – in the hope that someone will come by at some stage and clear away the garbage.

The Fine Art of Entertainment
The geishas of today

Whenever you even just mention the word "geisha", you are immediately suspected of talking in clichés. And usually this suspicion is correct. There is almost nothing else in Japan which has been illustrated, defined and explained so often, yet has still remained misunderstood.

So, for the purpose of thrashing out the endlessly discussed topic of geishas just a little more, let's cast our eye to Atami for a change and not to Kyoto, the actual home of the geishas. (Incidentally, in Kyoto they don't appreciate being called geishas, they prefer being referred to as *geiko*. But that's a different story.) In Atami we'll discover that life isn't always plain sailing, especially not for geishas.

In its heyday, Atami used to be so popular that it had the second-largest geisha community in the country, after Kyoto. At its peak there were almost 900 geishas living and working here. It is pretty certain that the geishas who were hired for the typical tourist parties, which could sometimes become quite excessive, were not expected to be as culturally refined as the vain geiko of Kyoto. When her refinement has reached perfection, she starts to become entranced, artificial, like something from a different planet. At this stage she is beyond the reach of normal human communication. And if I've understood it correctly, this is precisely what it's all about.

But the beer-swilling company parties in the city of 1000 lights didn't care for the fine art of reciting poems and singing songs, the fine, polished conversation and the perfect way of pouring sake anyway. And they still don't. The aim is to get drunk. During a proper geisha party all sorts of crude games are played where the "punishment" is inevitably alcohol. Consequently, in the end everybody is completely out of it, except for the geisha who never drinks when she is on duty. And as she often has more than one commitment during an evening, she might well disappear before the end of the feast to entertain another party of people somewhere else.

The geishas of Atami were always despised by their colleagues in Kyoto, if they bothered to acknowledge their existence at all. But although less cultural refinement was expected from them, they still were not spared the many years of hard training in song and dance plus the considerable expenses that go with the job. A good kimono costs anywhere between 30,000 and 50,000 euros. But

1 Absent looks, stylized dances. **2** Geishas on their way to work. **3** The facial expression is very important. **4** The future of this ancient art is looking rather bleak.

1 The professional clothes plus the wig cost several tens of thousands of euros. 2 Not every guest cherishes the performances. 3 Geisha performances for walk-in customers – maybe a way out of the crisis. 4 In the changing rooms – time for a chat and experiments with the new cell phone.

luckily they earn quite a lot. Their hourly rate is around 150 euros plus expenses and usually a nice tip on top. Of course a real *geiko* from Kyoto would not even put on her make-up for this paltry amount of money. They are much more expensive and exclusive, so their grace lends a certain cultural shine to the wild bonenkai, the popular, loud, drunken celebrations which are held at the end of the year. But things gradually changed in Atami. Morals went downhill, tastes become more and more basic and an increasing number of sex clubs and stripper joints opened up. As a consequence, many geishas ended up unemployed and their number decreased from 900 down to around 300. Those who weren't lucky enough to be kept or married by a faithful customer had to now earn their living as receptionists or waitresses.

Atami – the city of 1000 lights

The seaside resort Atami is about half an hour's train ride south-west of Tokyo. It used to be known as the "city of 1000 lights", but that's a while back now. It had its heyday during the 1980s. This was the time of the big economic "bubble", when every Japanese felt like a millionaire, money seemed to be growing on trees and was spent as carelessly as if it were confetti. Atami can safely be considered one of the symbols of those happy years. Thanks to its mild climate and its hot springs, Atami became the mecca for pleasure-seeking

employees. At that time the large companies took their re-sponsibility for their employees very seriously and paid for all sorts of jollies to keep the morale and commitment going. But then the 1000 lights went out, and suddenly the party was over and the golden years were succeeded by a long haul. Many companies were hit hard. As a consequence travel and entertainment budgets were reduced drastically. The luxury hotels of Atami stood empty. Many other centers of entertain-ment in Japan faced a similar fate. A huge number of the large entertainment parks and luxury hotels had been constructed under the assumption that this economic boom would go on forever and they had been built on a mountain of debts. Sud-denly they were caught in the whirl of recession and were forced to close down.

Out of desperation, the local trade association decided to allow the woeful old songs and dances to be performed in common theaters as well. Previously they had only been performed in the exclusive back rooms of expensive hotels. For male customers only, who were paying a lot of money for the pleasure. Now the performances are open to everyone. At any time. At the weekends or even in the morning. On the one hand this accelerated the demise of a highly respected and mysterious profession, but it also contributed to the democratization of this form of entertainment. Now suddenly women can enjoy the performances, too. Previously, the traditional geisha parties were strictly men's business.

When I speak of the "pleasure" of a geisha performance, I must warn you that it isn't exactly easy listening. Quite honestly, I don't think visi-tors from the West will be able to get any kind of pleasure from such a performance, unless it is a high-class geisha performance which can really be a cultural treat. But keep this our little secret, okay?

The Wild Wrestlers
The discipline of endurance

I have great pleasure in introducing you to a very different type of female entertainment which is almost unknown outside of Japan. It stands in stark contrast to the art of geisha entertainment, the oldest and most stubborn cliché of Japanese femininity. I am talking about professional female wrestling. In the home of sumo wrestling and karate, wrestling (or *purores* – short for our word pro wrestling) is serious business. Back in the '50's of the previous century the nation's blood boiled patriotically, when legendary Rikidozan bashed the notorious Sharpe Brothers from San Francisco to a pulp. This gave the Japanese, who suffer from a minority complex towards the US, a sorely needed boost to their ego. At the time they didn't know that Rikidozan was in fact of Korean descent. Up to fourteen million people all across the nation witnessed his triumph in 1954 on TV. It was celebrated as a Japanese miracle.

Of course female wrestling needed another few centuries before it became socially acceptable. Nagayo Chigusa was there from the start. Apart from entering the ring herself once a week, she runs an association of female wrestlers called "Gaea" and trains promising young newcomers.

But before we visit the training camp of the wild girls in Yokohama, we should get to know a very important – maybe the most important – Japanese verb: *gambaru.* It means "to hang in there, to endure". Even if you only spend a few days in Japan, you'll probably hear someone on the street or on TV call out *"gambare!"* or the politer form: *"gambatte kudassai!"* This is no less than the omnipresent encouragement to hang in there. "Grit your teeth!" "Don't give in!" This is an important sentiment in a country where a large part of social interactions consists of suppressing one another to define an order of hierarchy. Newcomers, whether at school, at university, at the sports club or at work, always have a hard time. The older ones, the ones that have been there for a while, are the *sempai* and the newcomer is the kohai. It goes without saying that the *kohai* has to obey all the *sempai's* orders. So you can imagine that the training of a professional female wrestler is one of the least pleasurable forms of education. And please note, although it may be hard to grasp at the beginning: the toughness and hardness is considered normal by everybody, unless it takes on a sadistic

1 Aya has to survive murderous sparring rounds… 2 …and hangs in there almost to the point of collapse. 3 "Dynamite Kansai" twists Nagayo Chigusa. 4 In the ring there is no mercy.

character – something which happens occasionally. Humiliation, persecution and many other nasty things we would consider torture do not evoke sympathy, let alone call out for Amnesty International, in Japan. The only thing they might provoke is an encouraging "Gambatte kudassai!" Only he who has survived the awful tortures will earn the respect of society. He will become a sempai himself and can start to have the pleasure of maltreating the *kohai* in precisely the same way that he was maltreated himself. This is the principle according to which a frighteningly large part of Japanese society works.

The rules of female wrestling are simple: two or more muscular women enter the ring together and try to beat the s… out of each other. The audience, amongst which there are also many young, but less muscular, females, encourages and applauds the gladiators, throwing paper streamers in the colors of their heroines into the ring. By watching the brutal and sometimes bloody fights they learn a couple of important lessons which help them survive in Japanese society. Number one: life is tough and unfair. Number two: you will receive respect and admiration if you dish out and

1 The audience celebrates its heroines with paper streamers in their colors. 2 Fantasy costumes and mean looks – a lot of it is pure show… 3 …but the pain is real. In no other country is female wrestling as tough as in Japan. 4 If you aren't well prepared, you can get injured badly.

Tough school: Nagayo Chigusa

She was born in Nagasaki in 1964 and originally wanted to study medicine. But as her parents couldn't support her endeavors, she turned to female wrestling. At that time, at the beginning of the 1980's, female wresting could still only be found in the dingy areas of the red light districts. Nagayo Chigusa and her ring partner, Lioness Aska, with whom she wrestled for many years, helped turn this sport into a serious and popular business. They were called the "Crush Gals". After the loss of a friend and colleague who died from brain injury following a fight, Nahayo swore that she would never

again let inadequately trained wrestlers climb into the ring. She has helped thousands of girls to catch the whiff of fame and honor and talks about her students with the loving pride of a mother. But she would never ever show these tender feelings to the girls. On the contrary, she behaves like a devil towards them. She screams at them, offends them and occasionally also hits them hard. Sometimes she comes home, she says, and cries, as the blows hurt her as much as her students. The aim of this tough training is to help the young wrestlers lose their fear and learn to hold their own in the ring. They are supposed to take the most important rules of female wrestling to heart: do not seriously injure anybody – but don't get injured yourself either.

endure a lot. These lessons are helpful for work, within the family and in relationships.

Aya, a young girl of 18, joined Nagayo Chigusa's camp to become trained as a professional wrestler. After being tortured for several months – six to eight hours a day, including fitness and weight training, training in how to fall properly, no visitors, no days off, she is finally tested in the ring. Now she has to prove that that she can survive a real fight against even the cruelest opponent. Throughout a whole afternoon, round after round, the more advanced team colleagues (her sempai) viciously check out her stamina and skills. They jump on her, push her over, kick her, punch her, pull her hair. She is battered around the ring like a rubber doll. She can only prove that she is ready for the ring if she gets up again and again and defends herself.

During the breaks her adored teacher Nagayo Chigusa screams at her, slaps her and humiliates her continuously. Aya could get up at any time and simply leave this shop of horrors. But she doesn't. And the reason why is the big secret of gambaru, a concept which every Japanese understands, but which is almost impossible to grasp for anyone outside the country. In Japan the biggest virtue is to overcome your weaknesses and imperfections and to become tough and enduring.

Finally Aya survives her debut fight – which she loses, of course. But that doesn't matter. The only thing that matters is that she stuck it out, didn't give in. The girls in the audience applaud and cheer like mad. In Japan it isn't too important to end up as the winner. The main thing is that you've made a real effort and have triumphed over yourself. The Japanese will always prefer a tragic loser, someone who makes mistakes and visibly suffers because of that, to a shining hero.

Gentle Giants
The sensitive bulls of Ojiya

From a lot of what I have described so far, it becomes apparent that the Japanese don't actively seek direct confrontation and fights, unless it is done in mutual agreement to entertain a paying audience, such as during a wrestling match. There are several other examples. After all Japan is home to various martial arts including judo, karate, sword fighting and sumo. Part of the magic of these disciplines is that two opponents measure their strength in a comparatively brutal way. But it is always done in a civilized, ritualized and polite manner. Maintaining respect and esteem for the opponent is the golden rule. Even during a sumo fight, the winner might throw his opponent to the ground roughly, but will maintain his dignity throughout. For instance it would be a taboo to jump on the opponent lying on the ground. In this country it is important to give the loser the chance to save his face. Apart from that it is vital that the overall harmony (wa) is not disturbed.

Since ancient times, when animals represented an early form of trucks, bullfights have always been held in Japan. Today they are only held in a few places. In Ojiya, Niigata prefecture, in Uwajima, in Shikoku and in Okinawa. Your first impulse might be to alert the Society for the Prevention of Cruelty to Animals. But if you have a closer look, you'll discover that these fights, too, are based on the deep and noble Japanese philosophy of maintaining harmony and respect. If you mention the Spanish bullfights to the bull keepers of Ojiya, they can become quite angry. They'll tell you, "That's disgusting." Presumably they love their bulls more than their wives and almost as much as the famous koi, the precious ornamental carp which are bred very successfully in Ojiya. They take care of their animals, stroke, feed and train them. They partake in their moods and can interpret their facial expressions. Late summer is the bullfighting season in Ojiya. At the weekends the proud farmers load their beefy gladiators onto their trucks and haul them up the mountain to the arena. They are mighty, frightening creatures. Horned mountains of muscles with worryingly alert eyes and the ability to growl like a lion. They weigh a

1 A bull rolling around on the ground – this is how they get a feel for the ring. **2** Eye to eye – the climax of every fight. **3** The audience is experienced and demanding. **4** The colossuses and their masters in the arena.

1 Although the bull has lost the fight, he is treated like a winner, so he doesn't get depressed. 2 Talking shop at the edge of the arena. 3 With a rope through the nose, every bull can be tamed… 4 …still, handling fighting bulls can be quite dangerous.

ton or more, yet allow their owners to lead them around on a rope as though they were lap dogs. First they are led into the arena, one after the other. The first thing they do here is roll around extensively in the sand. This looks a little silly, but the bull leaders assure me that this is important for them to get a feel for the territory which they are going to fight for later. Each bull has his own flag, which is stuck at the edge of the ring. The bullfights are a so-called national treasure. As such they receive financial support from the government. So whenever a bull is bought (the price for a promising bull is at least 7,000 euros), the Japanese tax-payers are involved as well. Still, no Japanese in his right mind would consider turning up to watch the spectacle. Apart from a few scattered tourists, the mountain people are usually left to enjoy the bullfights on their own.

As I said, it is a deeply Japanese competition. Its essence is expressed by a very fine and noble, almost chivalrous motto: no bull is injured and no bull wins. Of course a winner is declared at the end, the bull owners tell me, but the bulls should be oblivious to this as it would grieve them.

The owners treat their animals with a large amount of respect and address them with titles such as "Great Master". They bow before them and behave like their servants. They tell me that this flatters the bull's ego and makes it stronger.

When two bulls start charging at each other, the bull keepers make sure that they don't hurt, nor visibly and clearly defeat

A bull as a pet

Hirazawa Hidemasa, 19, a first-year student of economics, trains his four-year-old fighting bull, Chuzaemon, every day. He usually leads him to a fallen tree trunk which, after a lot of coaxing, the bull tries to lift it up with his horns. This strengthens his neck muscles. After training Chuzaemon is led back to his stable where he spends the rest of the day. Hidemasa tells me that here occasionally hens run around between his legs. This is good, as it keeps the bull alert.

Apparently bulls are afraid of hens. Chuzaemon is given three cloves of garlic a day to inspire his fighting spirit. On top of that his master mixes the dried skins of poisonous snakes into his food on the day before a fight. It is common knowledge that this makes bulls wilder. Apart from the fact that he is undoubtedly a bull, Chuzaemon is treated like a proper member of the family. His moods and desires are understood. "When he's happy, he bellows a strong mooooh," says Hidemasa. "But when he feels lonely, he can only utter a silent hmmhmm…"

each other. This has to be avoided, as the defeated bull would lose face. And then he would feel sad and would never fight again properly. In this respect bulls are like humans. Also, the character of the winner might be spoilt as well. The winning bull could possibly start to feel superior. In Japan such contemporaries, even if they are only bulls, are not welcome.

Therefore the bullfight is always broken off just before its climax, when the jury decides that one of the bulls has performed better than the other, without either of them having noticed it.

This is a real art which requires a lot of experience and knowledge of animal psychology. It also requires a good, strong hand to bravely grab the bull's nose at the right moment. This is the most effective method to quickly calm down even the wildest colossus.

Humility, Virtue and Fast Boats
Suffering and passion

It is not even 6 a.m. on a cool November morning in the north of Kyushu. The forecasts predict light rain, and it is still dark outside. It wouldn't exactly entice you to jump out of bed half naked, rush outside and proceed to rub yourself down with a wet towel, singing a merry song. But this is precisely what the morning program at the training center of the Japanese speed boat association looks like. First the trainees are woken up by military music. And look, there they are, running down the corridor – 76 boys and eleven girls, between fifteen and twenty years of age – slim, but athletic. There they go, out into the cold, standing in line to be counted. Then they rub themselves down with the aforementioned wet towel and proceed to do their morning exercises. The director of the school, Mr. Osaki, inspects the lines with a strict look on his face. His uniform isn't the only thing that appears military. This school is more like a barracks, only the recruits are not here to learn about how to fight a war. They are enjoying the one-year course to become a speed boat pilot. "We've got precisely one year to make professional speed boat pilots and valuable members of society out of these young people," Mr. Osaki says grimly. "That doesn't leave a lot of time for niceties."

Their education is in strict accordance with the motto "politeness and virtue", the ideal of Mr. Sasakawa Ryoichi who was the founder of Japanese speed boat racing. He was one of these businessmen with a vision who built whole business empires after the collapse of 1945. Like the other magnates, he was inventive, had a feeling for the market, enjoyed excellent political connections and was skilled. And he didn't even create a now product or sell anything. He made money out of the Japanese passion for gambling, in principle an illegal activity. But there are a few exceptions to this rule: horse, cycle and boat races. And you can also win cash at the ubiquitous *pachinko* game, although underhand. You need to take the detour of exchanging the little balls for prizes and the prizes for cash – to ensure that the whole thing stays legal.

After being released from prison in 1948, after he had been convicted for three years as a criminal of war, Mr. Sasakawa persuaded a few communities to allow boat races and to share the profits with him. Thus the Japanese speed boat association was born. It

1 Morning training at the crack of dawn. **2** Again and again – words of warning and lessons in between the races and exercises. **3** The light nutshells are easily out of control. **4** Often the race is already run during the first round.

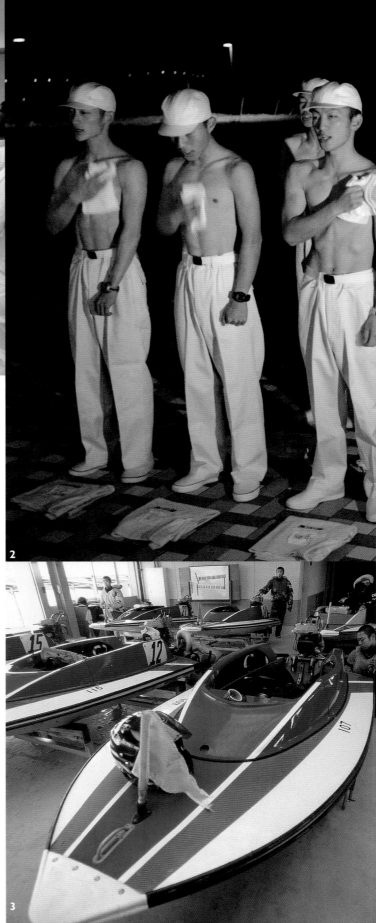

runs all the racing boat courses throughout the country plus all the betting shops. On top of that it owns the pilots and the boats. It is a flourishing business, as it has zero competition. The annual turn-over is several billion a year. And I mean dollars or euros, not yen! But it has to be said that the association does channel part of its profits into charitable projects. Mr. Sasakawa died in 1995 as the "richest fascist in the world", as he called himself once. He was an avid admirer of Mussolini, a passionate patriot and fan of the emperor and had the best connections to the underworld, which was also very faithful to the monarch. He was particularly interested in educating young people. This is why the hopeful young speedboat pilots who are trained at the center in Kyutu are taught military drill and iron discipline. If they survive this, they can expect pretty good salaries and prizes. After the morning roll call and before breakfast the trainees have to clean the barracks. Viennese waltzes blaring from the loudspeakers are probably supposed to sweeten this task. This early morning cleaning orgy is an exercise for the character which is widespread in Japan. We will come across it again later in the Zen monastery. This ritualistic cleaning is not only done to keep the place hygienic – the main aim is to help the kids develop a pure character and soul. While they are busy cleaning the boys and girls run around, they don't walk. They only stop, straighten up and bow with respect if they see one of their teachers.

After breakfast the national anthem is played. The loudspeakers ensure that it is heard right across the huge school grounds. Now everybody has to stand at attention: "Kimi-ga yo" ("May your reign last for 1000 years, until moss has grown over the

mighty rocks which today are still mere pebbles." – The emperor is meant.)

And then the kids hop into their boats and spend the entire day racing around at speeds of up to 80 kilometers per hour. They race around in a large circle. To the far marker and back, round and round it goes. The colorful demarcations are set 300 meters apart and look like lollipops. A race comprises three rounds, i.e., 1,800 meters. The races aren't terribly exciting, as it is clear who's going to win after the first round. In between races the trainees assemble again and again and stand at attention. They have to endure being humiliated by horrible teachers, have to lower their heads humbly and cry "Hai!" repeatedly. The poor trembling kid who caused a crash at the first marker and who fell into the

water is standing on the rescue boat, dripping wet, bowing to nothing the whole long way back to the start position. Let's rather not try to imagine what the rest of his day will pan out like. Next all the trainees have to take their motors apart completely and reassemble them again. The one who is slowest is punished by being put in detention. After dinner the trainees study speed boat theory for a couple of hours more, then they brood over the photographs of today's race rounds and analyze the results. And finally: "leisure time". Leisure time is spent in the common room watching boat races on TV. Visitors are not allowed. The mail is censored. Nothing will interfere with these young people and their aim.

Many Japanese – and not only those that are stuck in the past – firmly believe that such a tough military education full of humiliations and strictness is conducive to improving a person and encourages him to perform better. Even if, as is the case here, it is only about zooming around in circles in a small boat.

1 Like in a barracks: assembly for breakfast. **2** But before that, morning exercises and flag salute. In any weather. **3** The pilots look after their precious boats themselves. **4** Evening studies – all the trial races are analyzed in detail.

Until the Vocal Cords Give Out
Cheerleaders and the moments of power

Japanese student life is fun – especially at the highly reputed elite universities. Preparations for the entry exams start in the elite kindergartens. Compared to the hard slog and exam hell of school, universities are pure relaxation. The first four years of university up to graduation are easy. Whoever wants to and feels the vocation to can continue on and aspire to higher academic accolades. But for most it was usually enough to have graduated from the universities of Todai, Waseda, Keio or Hosei to sail straight into the elite professional life. Unfortunately the privilege of landing a great job immediately is no longer guaranteed due to the economic crisis which has been going on for the past few decades.

Whoever passes the entry exam to one of the universities doesn't need to spend much thought on intermediary exams and seminar essays. All he or she really has to do is to decide which working group to join. There are many of them: traditional cooking or English conversation, wrestling, jazz, big-band music or maybe *oendan*.

But if you choose this last group, life stops being fun. Japan's cheerleaders are the oen-dan. And if you envisage squealing girls hopping around in short skirts, you're only half right. Of course you've got them, too. And of course there's a brass band to cheer on the university team with peppy tunes. But the hard core of Japanese cheerleaders are the leaders themselves – a species of their own which you won't find anywhere else.

The leaders are always young men, no women – without exception. After they have been accepted to the club they are only ever seen in their stiff, black suits of a similar design to the school uniforms of Japanese boys. The leaders feel like the guardians of a holy tradition which has existed since the foundation of their university – usually in the late 19th century. This was a time when the Japanese started experimenting with baseball, which is the most popular sports discipline in the country until this day. The cheerleaders' biggest treasure is the university flag, which nobody else is allowed even to touch. The ceremonial display of this flag is the climax of each one of their performances. The leaders believe that they safeguard honor, etiquette and decency. They live in an isolated world of strict hierarchy and military drill. Newcomers have to be

1 Nothing is more holy to the cheerleaders than their university flag.
2 Baseball is Japan's national sport. **3** The cheerleaders always shout. They never speak in a normal tone of voice. **4** They scream and scream until they enter ecstasy – up to self-abandonment.

1 Group training in preparation for the match. 2 If the team scores, they do a triumphant dance. 3 Humiliation and submission – newcomers don't have much fun. 4 The audience obediently follows the cheerleader's cheering instructions.

completely submissive and humble and have to endure pain, humiliation and persecution without complaining. On the whole their world still describes the ideal of Japanese society: only through want and renunciation will you receive respect and influence.

An ineradicable pecking order determines life at Japanese universities (and many other institutions): during your first year you are treated like a nobody. During your second year you are treated like garbage. During your third year you are treated like an animal and only in your fourth year are you treated like a human being. So the younger students who weren't careful enough and joined an *oendan* have a tough time. They have to run around, work hard and serve. They address the older students in the most deferential terms the Japanese language has to offer. Orders and humiliations are barked at them as if they were dogs. They accept kicks and blows which would inspire us to murder fantasies and assassination plans. They bear it all, knowing that if they only stick it out *(gambaru)*, they will one day themselves be in a position to deal it out. Prior to any game of a university team, especially in spring when the six elite universities of Tokyo compete against each other, you

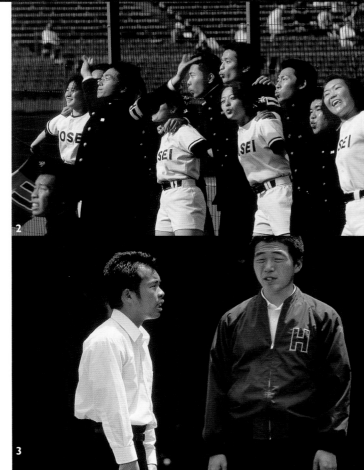

National sport number one

ou may think that baseball only arrived in Japan after World War II with the American occupation. But this isn't the case. Baseball came to Japan before that, during the meiji period (1868–1912). The government then was keen on finding out more about the life style in the west and to uncover the secrets of its perceived superiority. It supported baseball not only because it is good exercise, but also because it suits the Japanese team mentality. There is a clear hierarchy, everybody knows where his place is and where the game is easy to follow.

Yakyu (field ball) has been played professionally in Japan since the '30's. It then became the national sport when TV broadcasted it widely in the '50's. Today baseball has long left sumo wrestling behind as the favorite sport and is in no danger of being overtaken by soccer. Whether you have a look at the TV audience ratings, the newspaper coverage or the numbers of visitors to the matches – baseball is always number one. The best players are heroes for the kids who come to the matches at the weekends with their dads, clad in baseball uniforms Professional baseball players are also the highest paid advertising vehicles in Japan.

But the greatest fame and the highest honor is reserved for those players who manage to conquer the home of baseball and who play in the American Major League. At the moment they are Matsui Hideki (New York Yankees) and Suzuki Ichiro (Seattle Mariners). Their matches are always shown live and they feature as top news in the most important programs on TV several times a week.

Especially since nobody really fears the Japanese economic power any more, these two players support Japan's hope that they might be at least respected, particularly by the US.

they perform their grand *oen-dan* show and really manage to enthuse the audience.

The underlings are maltreated by their leaders, irrespective of whether it is boiling hot or pouring with rain. "Sometimes our novices faint," one of the top leaders told me. "But that doesn't matter. Those are the moments which you like to remember."

The leader's existence has other moments of pleasure. He can stand in the stadium and control the outbursts of hundreds, maybe thousands of fans who submit to his rules and rhythm voluntarily, as it is not their thing to scream or cheer spontaneously. When the rhythmical sounds of the big drums and the fanfares of the brass band heat up the people and the leaders show off their war dance and everyone is watching them and joining in – these are the moments of power which they never forget.

And it actually gives you a head start when applying for a job if you can prove that you were a member of an oen-dan. The potential employers prick their ears immediately, as they know that whoever has gone through this hell will not be frightened by anything any more. And he will certainly also be good at managing people. Well, at least he'll be good at the sort of people management that is still quite popular in Japan. And he will also have learnt to shout very loudly – which boils down to the same thing…

can watch the leader practice with his underlings somewhere near the stadium. They underlings are chased around and maltreated. It is heart-wrenching. They have to run to and fro hundreds of times in their black pants and boots, have to bow to their leader and endure his acid critique. He doesn't even turn around to address these worms. He just stands around with folded arms, looking disinterested and shouts out orders. "Not snappy enough, not in synchrony, not fast enough, not loud enough."

And then it is the big day of the game. The university anthem is blared out of tired throats. Tired, as the cheerleaders are not allowed to talk normally, they always have to shout. They spread their arms in a defined choreography which is based on movements from karate and kabuki. They look vaguely like air traffic controllers, directing an airplane rolling in to its park position. In doing this they embody the common image that we have of the fanatical and slightly strange Japanese. But in fact they are considered freaks in Japan, too. Only once a year they are not ridiculed, namely when

Soccer Without Goal and Offside
Holy pleasure at the game of Kemari

The Shirmane shrine in Kyoto was where the Asukai family lived in the 12th century. A family which was known for its poetry and its skill at playing kemari, the courtly form of soccer. When the spirit Sei-daimyojin, patron of ball games and fine arts, watched one of the old Asukais lifting the ball 1000 times, he offered to protect him and his family if he continued to focus his energy solely on the ball game. With this oldest known case of sport sponsoring, the long tradition of *kemari*, a mysterious and deeply Japanese sport, started. Why deeply Japanese? First of all because at the end of the game there is no nomination of winners and losers. Second of all because not even the most skilled player can rise in the team hierarchy if it isn't his turn yet. Performance and talent in Japan also has to obey the principle of seniority.

Today there are only about 30 *kemari* enthusiasts left in the country. They meet up for a match ten times a year at certain feast days. Once a year they meet up at the Shirmane shrine for that purpose. By the way some people with a lot of imagination claim that *kemari* is an early form of soccer.

Putting on the splendid costumes and the black wooden clogs, which were specially designed for the game in the 13th century, has its own ritual. The color of the costume signifies the rank of the player. The game leader, Onishi Yasuyosi, who wears bright pink himself, explains that there are 60 ranks. Each one of these ranks has to be purchased by buying a certificate. In olden times mainly the emperor's house happily earned money from this procedure, as it was the authority issuing the certificates.

A Japanese passion, way beyond the soccer grounds, is refinement right down to the smallest detail and a strict unchangeable set of traditional rules and stylized processes. On first sight many of them seem rather involved and don't seem to serve any other purpose than to confirm the authorities and hierarchies. This principal is called *kata*. It describes the defined and undisputable form with which something has to happen because this is the way it is and always has been. It reaches a climax in the tea ceremony and in various bureaucratic processes. The heart of the *kemari* game is the ball. At least this is one thing this game has in common with many other ball games we are familiar with. The kemari ball weighs only 120 grams and is a work of art made of deer and horse leather. The side parts which are made of soft

1 Classic temple dances set the frame. 2 The Shiramine shrine in Kyoto. 3 The ritual of getting dressed in the valuable costumes for the game. 4 The ball is treated with utmost respect before it is kicked.

1 Kick-off — no jury is needed, as there is no winner. **2** The gentlemen kick the ball to and fro while chanting to the gods. **3** Before the match begins, the players and the balls are blessed. **4** The hierarchy is strict — each rank has its own color.

deer leather are sewn together by a band of elastic horse leather. The balls are treated with utmost respect and are carried around in wooden boxes when they aren't being kicked. During the game the players are only allowed to touch it with their right foot and only with an out-stretched leg. After the players have honored the god of the balls in a Shinto ceremony and have prayed for peace and a good harvest, and following a performance of courtly dances in the pavilion, the players take their positions on the playing field. With endlessly slow steps Mister Onishi carries the holy ball to the middle of the playing field. Then the kick-off: the ball flies from one player to the next twice, three times. Throughout the game the players beseech the gods with long chants. Then the ball lands on the ground, is picked up again and a new round begins. After just over fifteen minutes and after a secret sign has been given the players somehow agree that this is enough now. They retreat from the playing ground the same way they arrived — humbly and dignified.

Music from a different time

The *sho* is the mouth organ of Japanese courtly music. It is also used during the intro to a game of *kemari*. It consists of a cup-shaped wind chamber body with 17 pipes extending from the top of it. Two of these pipes don't make a sound. (I am sure there'll be a Japanologist who will be able to explain why in detail and write a book about it.) By inhaling and exhaling, the sho player produces a continuous sound with several tones. The sound is so old and so strange to our ears that I

always get goose bumps when I hear it, as to me it sounds like a call from another time.

The repertory of courtly music goes way back to the Chinese T'ang dynasty (618–907) and has Indian and central Asian influences as well. Apart from the sho, the instruments of a chamber orchestra include a whistle, which is a little like an oboe and produces a penetrating sound, and three kinds of flutes. Then there are one or more string instruments and drums which are drummed in a rhythm known only to the drummer. The music is slow and solemn and not exactly catching.

Looking for the Superstar
The desire for acknowledgement

The preceding chapters illustrate that the Japanese are hard to beat in their love for competition and their almost limitless wealth of imagination regarding the invention of new, entertaining or bizarre disciplines in which the competitors have the opportunity to measure their strength and skill.

This doesn't come as a surprise, as the majority of Japanese childhood and youth is marked by entry exams for kindergartens, schools and universities. Those who haven't adopted competitive thinking at some stage are usually outsiders. Many Japanese have this urgent need to prove themselves, to rise above the rest and to earn respect through exceptional performance. There is probably no other country in the world where more certificates are issued, more prize cups are handed out (and more certificates adorn the living rooms and more cups are exhibited in the cupboard) than in Japan. The point is to prove that that particular person is someone special. But then on the other hand we keep on hearing this saying with reference to Japanese society: the nail that sticks out needs to be hammered in so that it is in line with the others. But that's not necessarily a contradiction. Especially by finding ways of competing with each other, the Japanese have an unconventional, but functional, vent for their talents and desires. There are countless competitions including some that we are familiar with, such as photo competitions and dance competitions. The Japanese also have eating competitions, screaming competitions, fighter robot competitions, wrapping up and snow digging competitions, deer-food-throwing competitions and hair-growing competitions – and he who cannot enter into the latter due to lack of resources can join a shiny-bald-head competition. There are poetry, calligraphy and English competitions. There is even a which-pet-looks-most-similar-to-its-owner competition, plus many more. Everybody is particularly good at something, maybe better than others, and he or she is encouraged to demonstrate this. I would like you to rethink the common statement that the Japanese do not understand the concept of individuality and feel most comfortable in the anonymous, homogenous mass and hate to stick out. We should never forget that karaoke was invented in Japan. No nation who is capable of such an invention can

1 Well aimed – the snowball championship in Hokkaido. 2 Eat-Beef-Shout-Loud competition in Kyushi – he who shouts loudest wins.
3 Crying sumo – a competition for the tiniest. 4 Modern ballroom dancing – a passion of many Japanese

1 o hit the opponent and not to be hit oneself – the main rule of the snowball championship. 2 Shake the baby about until it finally cries. Pinching is forbidden. 3 The ice barricades which are set up on the playing field come in handy. 4 At the robot competition, young constructors let their fantasy monsters fight against each other.

be fundamentally interested in anonymity and submersion in a faceless mass or group. Although the group offers comfort and protection, you can leave it any time, at least playfully.

In January each year a particularly quirky tournament which is worthwhile visiting is held in the snowy winter landscape of the northern island of Hokkaido. It is held in the small town of Sobetsu, in the shadow of a small, smoking volcano, the Show-Shinzan, which appeared quite by surprise in the middle of a vegetable field in 1943.

For the International Snowball Championship each team is provided with 90 hard snowballs and has three minutes to try to hit as many players of the competing team as possible, whilst being hit as little as possible. The opponents hide behind walls and fire back, ducking and diving so as not to be hit. But that is

Naki-zumo: The first cry wins

The *naki-zumo,* the crying competition, is as old or almost as old as sumo itself. This competition is carried out at many shrines throughout the country. Like sumo, the *naki-zum* is a fight which is deeply connected to religious traditions. This is how it goes. The proud parents bring their children, which were born the year before, and hand them to overweight strangers. Usually, as the babies are fixated on their moms, they start to cry. That's a good thing, as according to an old Japanese saying only a screaming

baby is a healthy baby. Therefore the baby that is first to cry has won.

At the Sensoji Temple in Tokyo's district of Asakusa on the last Sunday in April, every year, the sweet little kids are laid into the massive hands of live sumo wrestlers. Strictly speaking they are members of the sumo working group of Tokyo University. In any case they lift the babies up, shake them and swing them around to achieve the desired result. But that's not enough for some babies. The rules dictate that if none of the rivaling babies starts to cry within 60 seconds, the dignified ring judges rush over and scare the babies with devil masks. This is too much for any baby to bear.

Of course this raises the question whether they don't fear that they might traumatize their kids for life.

"Surely not", one of the child scarers told me. "Nowadays no kid is afraid of the old Japanese devils. The little ones are used to much worse on TV." But it certainly prepares them for a life of competitions. It seems like you cannot start early enough with this.

not really the point. The main thing is that everyone has a good time and in the end the happy winner receives a prize and a certificate for his living room wall and cupboard.

Always Something to Admire
Japan's seasons

Apart from a few nasty typhoons, Japan's climate is temperate and, thanks to the immense size of the country, extremely varied. From the northernmost tip of Hokkaido to the southern Ryukyu Islands the country embraces several climatic zones. Projected onto a European map, Japan would extend from the Alps to the southern Sahara. Tokyo would be on the level of Tunis and Sapporo would be on the level of Rome.

In winter the part of the Japanese islands which faces the continent is buried under a blanket of snow three to four meters deep. The snow is brought by the icy air from Siberia. Over the Sea of Japan this cold air gets saturated with humidity and dumps its weight over the slopes of the Japanese Alps. In Tokyo on the other hand you hardly ever see snow. It is only two hours by car away, but is located behind the mountains. Here the winter days are dry as a bone with clear, clear blue skies and temperatures which rarely drop below zero. Then spring arrives with an explosive power and beauty. Unfortunately it is only short-lived and gives way to an oppressively hot summer which cools down when the typhoon season starts in September. But this doesn't mean that you can't have tropical storms as early as May, moving in a northerly direction, accompanied by downpours of rain and stormy winds. At the bottom of their heart the Japanese are closely tied to nature. Their seasons are very clear and distinct, and each one has its own special magic which poets have written about ever since they learnt how to write and which has moved painters and woodcut artists more than any other motive. The Japanese make an effort to consciously experience spring, summer, fall and winter. Each season has its own motifs, dishes, plants, scents and clothes, its own festivities and entertainments, and its own colors. Not only the emergence of seasonal dishes, but also the fixed sequence of blossoms are national events. There is not a single daily newspaper which doesn't regularly keep its readers informed about where this and that flower is currently most beautiful. And the news on TV also rarely dismiss their viewers without images of nature. First the plum blossom delights the nation, the cherry blossom comes next. This blossom receives special attention. It is a key topic of every weather report. The path of the blossom season is tracked carefully. The first

1 The colors of the Japanese forests in fall are enchanting. **2** Spring feelings – the plums start off the blossom season. **3** The "Sakura front" wanders from south to north. **4** Rowing on a sea of cherry blossoms – in the moat of the Emperor's Palace.

cherry blossoms appear down south in Kyushu in late March. In Hokkaido the cherry tree doesn't do its thing before mid-May. The cherry blossom season is important, as it sets the date for the hanami.

From September on the cold air masses which hid in the north throughout the summer start to move southwards, down the long archipelago, transforming the forests into breath-taking works of art.

The most colorful trees are the maple trees with their glowing red leaves and the gingko trees with leaves turned yellow. Nowhere in Japan is fall more beautiful and festive than in Kyoto with its approximately 2000 monasteries and temples. When the November leaves surround the pavilions and prayer halls and create splashes of color in the gardens of the tea houses and transform the hiking trails through the surrounding mountains into a red carpet of leaves, then we are struck again, as during the cherry blossom season, by this deep feeling of transience — of beauty which cannot last.

Hanami or the shortness of life

Hanami means "blossom show". According to old scriptures hanami started at a cherry blossom party held by General Toyotomi Hideyoshi in 1598. The General invited his friends and comrades to sit under the pink blossoms, write lovely poems and drink a lot of sake to celebrate the fact that he had succeeded in conquering the entire country. Today nobody needs a particular occasion to spread out the blue plastic sheets in the parks, unpack lots of beer, sake and snacks, and submit to this biggest pleasure of spring. The

first visitors appear early in the morning. They are sent by their company or university to reserve the best spot. Towards lunchtime it gets fuller and fuller and by afternoon you can hardly squeeze through the masses of people. They sit together until late into the night looking up at the blossoms which are lit up romantically. The main hanami center in Tokyo is the largest park of the city in Ueno. The park is 626,000 square meters large and boasts 1,100 cherry trees. Another place to enjoy this event is *Shinjuku Gyoen* which has 1,500 cherry trees, including 75 different varieties.

Hundreds of thousands of people sit together in a happy picnic mood, play music and mess around, look up at the blossoms in awe, or fall asleep after too much drink.

Since ancient times cherry blossoms have been revered mainly due to their ephemeral beauty. They are the idealized short version of our life on Earth which will undoubtedly end with a fresh breeze which will suddenly blow us off the tree of life. Like a cherry blossom.

Fall is the peak season in Kyoto. During this time the city is packed. If you haven't booked months in advance, you won't find anywhere to stay. The hotels, newspapers and TV report on the degree of red of the trees in the various temple gardens and continuously keep the fall foliage tourists up to date on what's happening.

1 By mid-November the colorful fall leaves have hit Kyoto. **2** Siberian winds deposit their load of snow over the west coast of Japan. **3** In April the Japanese wander under a canopy of blossoms.

Japan's flowers – The camellias (**1, 5, 9**) sweeten the winter. The azaleas (**7**) blossom after the cherry trees. Then the hydrangeas (**3**) display their colors, encouraged by the rainy season. Then it is the hibiscus's (**2**) and the lilies' turn (**4, 6**), such as in the Meiji garden (**8**), just next door the wild flowers in the Yoyogi Park (**10**). In fall the cosmea comes to flower (**11**) and so it goes. Japan is a country of flowers.

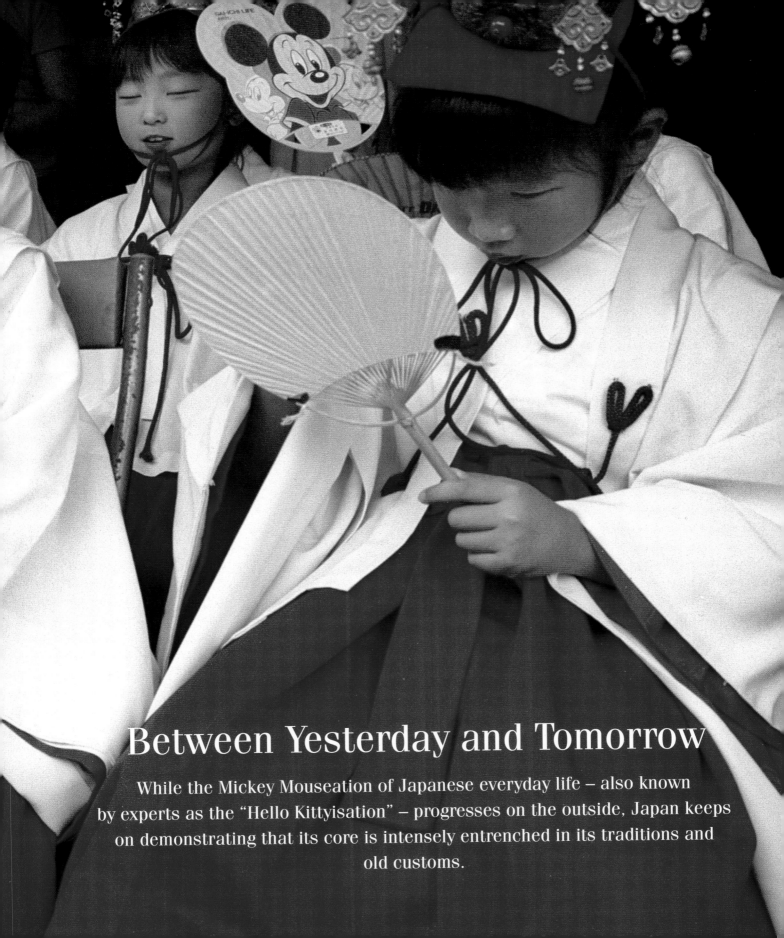

Between Yesterday and Tomorrow

While the Mickey Mouseation of Japanese everyday life – also known by experts as the "Hello Kittyisation" – progresses on the outside, Japan keeps on demonstrating that its core is intensely entrenched in its traditions and old customs.

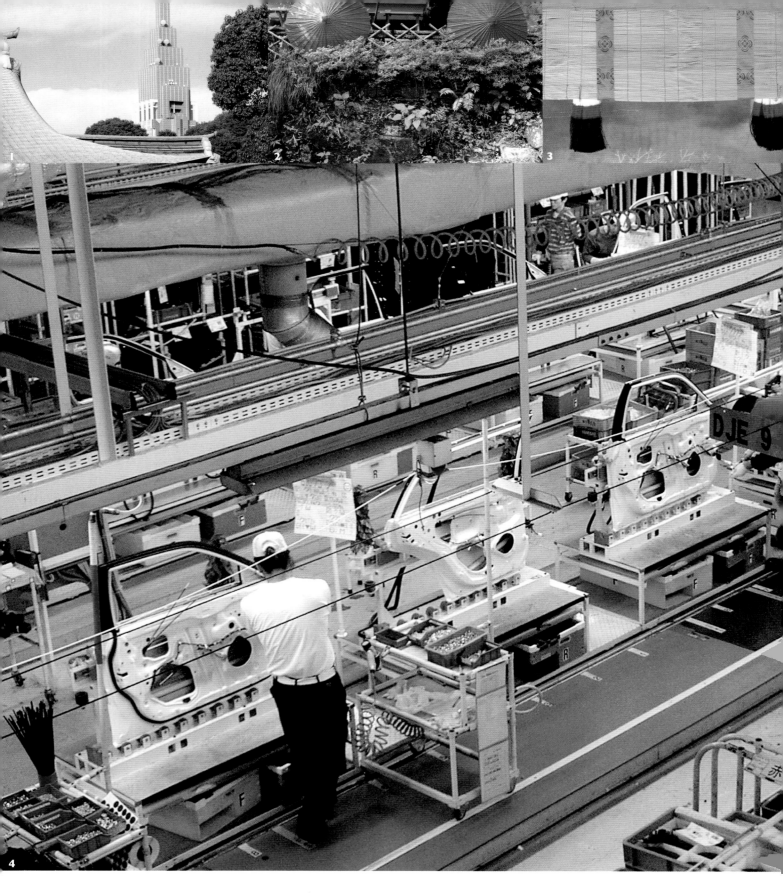

Of Tradition and Curiosity
Modern corporate Japan

A firm prejudice about the Japanese, one also kept alive by the Japanese themselves, is that of their proverbial working craze. Regularly the numerous cases of *karooshi*, death by over-working, find their way into our media and horrify us. But that isn't quite fair. Yes, the Japanese do work more hours than we do, but they also earn more. And, yes, they do have fewer holidays than we do, on average fifteen days, which as we know they don't always take. But rarely has anyone made the effort to add on their public holidays — they have at least a handful more than we do. Nobody ever points out that the first five days of a new year are almost automatically considered a holiday, that at the end of April/beginning of May during the "golden week" (with three public holidays) whole factories close down and that around August 15 on the Buddhist feast for the ancestors, o-bon, or during the cherry blossom season or if there is a matsuri in the community, working hours are very flexible. There must therefore be other reasons for the rise of this country as an economic power. It can't only be the famed fanatical work morale of its inhabitants.

However, Japan's economic sheen has paled meanwhile. The country was punished with a long and bitter recession for its risky excesses in the times of the "bubble". Banks collapsed, companies went bust and even large corporations had to cut down on their number of employees. Debts grew and grew, and the rest of the world, which had just been ruminating full of awe and worry on the introduction of Japanese management concepts, was relieved to find that in the end corporate Japan faces the same problems as every other country. Suddenly this country, whose economic health had been held in such high esteem, had to find ways out of high unemployment rates, while in the parks of the large cities the tent villages of the homeless started to sprawl and the crime rate rocketed. Suddenly Japan was no longer the island of happiness. And although it is still the second largest economic power in the world, it is gradually disappearing in the shadow of up-and-coming, ambitious China.

Japan has to reinvent itself, and I am sure it will manage. For instance Japan's automotive industry quickly picked up again after

1 Neighbors in Tokyo: the Meiji shrine and the high-rise office building of NTT DoCoMo. **2** A tea garden in Kamakura. **3** Clear lines, a few blotches of color — simple aesthetics. **4** The automotive industry on the upswing — the Toyota factory in the city bearing the same name, near Nagoya.

several painful changes in course had to be taken. At the start of the millennium most car manufacturers were in a better position than ever, with profits at an all-time high.

My explanation for this is the curiosity of the Japanese and their ability to rapidly analyze the new and unknown and to take over useful and helpful things straightaway and make them their own. They are not the least bit shy in the face of new developments, especially with regard to technical developments. They continuously dream of new inventions, above all of robots, and embrace progress, while we brood over any development for ages, wondering how a new development may fit in with the working hours we are used to and the norms of the European Union. We cogitate on whether it may cause harm and whether in the long term it may endanger the breeding areas of quail. Japan is simply faster and more persistent and, if necessary, more brutal. And thanks to its culture, which is based on arriving at a consensus, there is the guarantee that a new direction will be adopted smoothly, once a structural decision has been made.

Japan draws its strength, including its economic strength, from its traditions much more than we do. As opposed to us, the Japanese do not consider their traditions as outdated, old-fashioned or obso-

lete, they consider them a vibrant part of their everyday life. The old and traditional is not shoved to the side and run over. It continues to exist.

Let's take their fisheries and rice cultivation as an example. Two pillars of food for the country. They are generally run in just the same

1 Family-run businesses feed the country, such as these fishermen in Wakasa Bay... 2 ...and rice farmers harvesting in Kyushu. 3 The archer's new year's parade at the Meiji Shrine, Tokyo. 4 Sunday in the park: a lesson in playing the Australian didgeridoo. 5 The fascination of future technology: the Japanese aren't afraid of robots. 6 The cliché of the work-crazy Japanese does not always fit. 7 Camping area for the banished: the homeless live in tents in the park.

way as they always have: by family-run businesses and small cooperatives. Or the traditional handicrafts. It is quite possible that on one of your walks through the eastern part of Tokyo you will come across an old kite-maker right next to that garishly lit-up 24-hour shop. He would have learnt his trade from his father and would somehow still be running his shop.

But probably Japan's most important tradition is to remain completely open to new impulses from outside. There is probably no other nation which is as enthusiastic and willing to accept foreign influences and to experiment with them. It doesn't matter whether it is belly dancing, French cuisine or the didgeridoos of the Australian aborigines. In our immediate neighborhood in Tokyo we have a store selling Turkish carpets, an old and established specialist store offering a spectacular choice of walking sticks, an importer of old, disused American gasoline pumps, vending machines for chewing gum and neon ads for "Budweiser", a Danish baker and a Hong Kong noodle restaurant, a store stuffed full of model tanks and airplanes from World War II which you can assemble yourself (the shop is called "German Hobby" as many Japanese still believe that Germans love any form of militarism), a butcher whose ham is so good it brings tears to our eyes and a chocolate store called

"Musée de Chocolat" which sells the most heavenly chocolates, tarts and cakes.

But those who claim that Japan is completely Westernized are totally wrong. On the contrary, I believe that Japan is quite resistant to the trends in globalization, as globalization already started here 100 years ago. Not because multi-national corporations were driving it, but because the Japanese always were hungry, curious and ready for things that other cultures and nations could offer to enrich their lives.

But that does not mean that Japan is keen on immigrants and foreigners. No, surely not. They prefer to stay amongst themselves. There are only two million registered non-Japanese in this country of 127 million. This is a tiny proportion. And of these two million non-Japanese most are Koreans who have been living here since generations but who still haven't been granted citizenship. On the political side, too, no efforts are being made to increase the proportion of foreigners in this country, although demographically it would not only be a good idea, but is necessary.

But the curiosity and desire for the foreign is there. The Japanese want to absorb it and adapt it to their own needs. This is what happened with Buddhism and Chinese writing, with Western architecture and literature and with the hamburger. But: if foreign things are to be successful and lasting, then they need to be adapted to Japanese rules and needs. So for instance a hamburger might need to be turned into a *teriyaki* burger, or else it won't survive long in this country.

1 Old handicrafts persist – a kite-maker. **2** The signs of the yakuza, the Japanese mafia, are their tattoos.

Human advertising

The Japanese economy has achieved its most spectacular successes thanks to its highly developed advertising culture. You'll hardly find an empty space on the fronts of the buildings in the business districts or in the subway stations which

doesn't serve as a space for neon ads and colorful bills and posters. The variety of new products which swamp the market is incredible. Just the variety of soft drinks – from peach-carrot juice to designer water – is overwhelming! As a consequence Japanese consumers have long become immune to the garish ads, out of a sense of self-protection or weariness. That's why retailers and the entertainment industry grab the megaphone and send friendly, but persistent, young people out onto the streets to distribute packs of tissues or coupons. Or else they throw human advertising pillars into the battle with the almost impossible job of attracting attention. Incidentally there is no lack of applicants for such jobs: a substantial portion of the Japanese youth spends its best years as so-called *freeter*, going from one casual job to the next.

In the Footsteps of the Ancestor
The horse festival in Soma and the very last Samurai

Once a year, at the end of July, the women of the small town of Soma in the prefecture of Fukushima sense a strange change in their men. They suddenly become stricter, more determined — somehow more manly. The reason for this is that the time for the *soma nomaoi* is approaching. This is the great horse festival where the Samurai, the warriors of feudal Japan who are revered until today, come to life for a weekend.

In medieval times, mountainous Fukushima was a region marked by battles. Hostile neighboring clans, the Soma and the Date, waged war against each other and hired thousands of warriors for support. Therefore the probability of coming across a descendent of a Samurai in this region, 300 kilometers northeast of Tokyo, is higher than anywhere else in Japan.

Of course you wouldn't spot them right away. Nowadays they are clerks and bus drivers, shopkeepers, craftsmen and jewelers. But once a year, at the end of July, they take their suits of armor and their banners, which have been family treasures for generations, out of the wardrobe for the "Festival of the Wild Horses", the *soma nomaoi*. Then they climb onto their horses to go back in history, to get back in touch with their ancestors for a weekend. You get a feel for the spirit of the festival from the start. The festival is opened by a magnificent parade of 500 riders in full Samurai armor riding through the town center. The spirit of the festival continues — and the horse race looks authentic, too: all riders are dressed in full war gear, holding up banners proudly. Another highlight is the flag chase, where a flag is shot high up into the air and the riders have to try and catch it. Whoever manages to grab it in the midst the mass of horses and armor achieves fame for himself and his family.

You will hardly find prouder and grimmer Japanese than at this festival. Staring straight ahead, looking quite fearsome, they ignore the oppressive heat of July — sweating under the 35-kilogram weight of their armor, their helmets and wigs made of horse hair — and navigate their unwilling, nervous horses through the crowd of spectators with a sure hand. They shout at each other in deep, angry voices even if they are showing respect. It sounds rough and authoritarian — what else do you expect from a Samurai?

1 Mr. Tachibana decorating his hired horse for the festival of Soma.
2 Each helmet bears a heraldic animal. 3 The festival commission waiting for the parade. 4 They want to appear proud and grim — clerks turn into heroes when they wear their armors.

Of course in Europe we have got our knights, too. But here they have retired. They merely stand around in the corners of old castles collecting dust and spider webs. The same applies to their history.

In Japan on the other hand not a day will pass where you won't find at least one Samurai drama on TV. Sword-wielding heroes and villains with glowing eyes and strange hairdos charging at and slashing each other. And finally the tragic hero delivering a heart-wrenching monologue once more, where he vows that nothing, not even his love to his woman, will interfere with his duties as a Samurai.

Since the early 10th century, the Samurai controlled the military and political scene in Japan by a system which was similar to Europe's feudal system. As vassals of their feudal lords (daimyo), they enjoyed several privileges, including having land and serfs of their own. As long as there was war and unrest in the country, the livelihood of several hundreds of thousands of warriors was secured. But when the Tokugawa shogunate was established in 1603, including stable nationwide control, there wasn't much to conquer and pillage anymore. This is when the proud warriors suffered from a serious identity crisis. They were no longer needed. They either settled in the shadows of the castles where their lords were still having a good time, or they became tax collectors, guardians, defenders of the law, bureaucrats or gangsters. Some retired, others were caught gambling and were constantly involved in brawls, and still others tried to become businessmen and fine gentlemen.

Interestingly it was precisely during this time of idleness that the romantic Samurai philosophy of loyalty, honor and self-abandonment developed. It is also known as *bushi-do* — the path of the warrior. This philosophy has determined the idealized image of this class — both in Japan and abroad. Every kid knows the story of the 47 ronin (this is what those Samurai are called who have lost their lord, their employer, and as a consequence also their meaning of life). After their patron was murdered, these 47 ronin pretended to be completely demoralized and destitute, going to bits completely, giving themselves up. But as soon as everyone had lost respect for

The last armor-makers

Mr. Tachibana Satoshi from Soma is one of only four crafts-men in the country who still continue the old art of making armors. The armor of a Samurai is made up of approximately 10,000 individual parts of hard leather and metal. It consists of ten main elements: the chest plate, arm and leg protection, and so on. A well-preserved Samurai armor is worth several tens of thousands of euros. Mr. Tachibana hardly ever builds new armors. That would be far too expensive anyway. He is kept extremely busy mending and restoring the old armors. His ancestors were Samurai as well and he complains bitterly about the loss of the chivalrous spirit. "I always tell my children: when you're old like myself, this country will have long gone to the dogs."
Tom Cruise would be honored if he knew that his film The Last Samurai touched Mr. Tachibana deeply. He admitted that he cried four times in the cinema.

them and had quit fearing them, they sought noble revenge for the murder.

Of course you rarely hear the less uplifting stories from the medieval times, particularly of the suppressed, a mass of farmers with no rights whatsoever, who weren't even allowed to have a surname. The warriors were the only ones who had the right to carry weapons and to hack at anybody just passing by merely to test the sharpness of their swords.

When at the onset of modern times and when American war ships arrived in Japan the proverbial jolt went through the country and everything was supposed to change, the warriors (especially those in the south) initially rebelled against the rigid shogunate, but then also (particularly those from the north) against the new and completely non-Japanese morals. But eventually they were quashed by the merciless modern times and its superior weapons. – This is the stuff from which the epic dramas of heroes are made of.

Many of the enthusiastic participants at the *soma nomaoi*, the "Festival of the Wild Horses", can prove that their great-great-

grandfathers fought in the Samurai war of Fukushima in 1868, in which the Samurai had gone to war to defend the Shogun. It was the so-called boshin civil war. But they were defeated. To this day their descendents carry their flags with great pride and feel this almost holy tremor once a year. Where they pretend that time has stood still. And they dream of the days where honor, courage and faithfulness still meant something.

1 This warrior is taking a break with a beer. **2** Two Samurai as traffic controllers. **3** The parade of the 500 warriors. **4** When the red flag drops, the riders go berserk.

1

2

3

9

Politicians and Cement Heads

How to win an election

It would be completely naïve to expect any politician in this country to do anything about the lax noise-control laws. Politicians of any conviction and party create more noise than anybody else. Yes, even more than the guy selling bamboo washing-line rods. And they make the most noise shortly before elections. Political candidates cruise around the streets in their busses, from morning to night, with loudspeakers mounted on their roofs. Wearing white gloves they wave to the potential voters scurrying away or to houses and mountains. And they repeat their name as often as possible in the hope that it somehow gets stuck and leads to that desired vote on the ballot paper.

The candidate Gotoda Masazumi (motto: "we can") from the district of Tokushima 3 on the island of Shikoku follows the same strategy. Only he has hired a woman with a penetrating voice to call out his name for him. She cries out as though she were announcing the Messiah himself: "Be happy, dear citizens, the candidate Gotoda is here. Yes, it is the real candidate Gotoda in person. Thank you for welcoming him so warmly." The fact that there isn't always a warm welcome for him doesn't matter. The candidate makes sure of a lot of cordiality himself by hopping out of his jeep in every village and rushing around shaking hands. His hands are in bandages already, and each handshake causes horrible pains. Alas, throughout the world election campaigns are not for the weak or hesitant. Mr. Gotoda – who jogs through the communities and greets stunned old ladies, enters offices without invitation, and then hops back into his jeep and disappears again – is a candidate for the Liberal Democrats, the LDP. Since the day this party was established, it has been ruling modern-day Japan. There were only two small interruptions – which are hardly worth mentioning – throughout all this time. Why are they so successful? Partly because the members of the opposition seem to be on a continuous mission to rip each other to pieces and hardly present themselves as an attractive alternative for the voters. But the other reason for the success of the LDP is that Japan's majority voting system gives rural votes much more weight than urban votes – sometimes double as much. So it comes as no surprise that the LDP has traditionally

1 The district of Tokushima is idyllic, but economically underdeveloped. 2 Cement and concrete are the curse of rural Japan. 3 Only rarely is nature left to run its own course. 4 Election campaign in Japanese: candidate Gotoda Masazumi races from one village to the next waving at the local population.

tried to keep up good relations with the rural population. Therefore the promises that Mr. Gotoda croaks out with a hoarse voice relate mainly to the allocation of further public money to improve the regional infrastructure. These promises always convince the voters that he is the right man. The people of Tokushima, a beautiful region without much industry, are dependent on the public contracts. Road and bridge construction. Maybe another anti-landslide wall here? Maybe another dam there? And what about a new tunnel?

There is no country in the world, and certainly none with such a spectacular natural environment, which covers itself with concrete as much as Japan does. Japan's coasts are protected by tetrapods and walls, its mountain slopes disappear under gray layers of concrete and almost no river meanders along its natural course. The wild and life-threatening forces, such as the earthquakes, the tsunamis, the typhoons, the heavy downpours, the landslides and volcanic eruptions, are only partly responsible for this. To a large extent the

The first Asian parliament

The Japanese parliament, the first in Asia, convened in 1890 for the first time. As it was an emperor's parliament at that time, of course it didn't have any say. Only in 1947, in line with the new constitution, did it receive the authority to draft laws. The imposing granite structure of the parliament building built in 1936 dominates the government district Kasumigaseki near

the Emperor's Palace in the center of Tokyo. The parliament has two chambers, the House of Lords and the House of Commons. The House of Lords has little power, especially as its decisions in all important areas can be wiped away by the House of Commons with a two-thirds majority. As the LDP has held the majority in both houses since time immemorial there are seldom any surprises, and the Chairman of the LDP has also always automatically been the Prime Minister. And he is fully aware that his actual enemies are not to be found in the rows of the powerless opposition, but in the various wings of his own party. Therefore he always has to strive for balance and harmony. This drains a large part of his energy. Meanwhile governmental business is run by a Kafkaesque bureaucracy. Decisions are routinely signed off by the individual ministers, who usually haven't got a clue.
And throughout they talk about necessary reforms with great enthusiasm, just as we do…

1 The villages in Tokushima face the problem of city migration. **2** And another bit of concrete in the mountains. **3** Gotoda Masazumi making friends with young voters. **4** He promises equal living standards. **5** They trust him, because his uncle sat in parliament.

power politics of the LDP are responsible for this development, and in Tokushima they don't even make a secret out of this. The boss of the local construction company who has been busy maintaining a 1.5 kilometer stretch of road for the past 10 years tells me, "For us there is no alternative to Gotoda – 70 to 80 percent of us are dependent on the public contracts."
No less than 10 percent of the national budget in 2003 alone was poured onto mountains, into valleys and along coasts in the form of cement – 65 million euros. And that is substantially less than in previous years. Maybe this is because the areas of land which haven't yet been cemented in and hedged in are becoming smaller and smaller. Japan is certainly not becoming more beautiful in the

process – and not really any safer either. But the workplaces in rural areas which are structurally weak are secured and the LDP is re-elected. "We have to ensure that the same living standards are maintained throughout the country." This is how Mr. Gotoda defends the cement craze of the politicians. Of course he doesn't mention the almost endless possibilities of this system of give and take which has developed between the powerful construction lobby and the bureaucrats of the ministries. Let's assume that he simply doesn't know anything about it.
Incidentally, he was re-elected by a great majority. What helped was that people fondly remembered his uncle, another Mr. Gotoda, who had sat in parliament for years and years. Japanese voters are grateful voters and are willing to transfer their loyalty to the sons and daughters, nieces and nephews of the politicians they like. A large number of all Japanese delegates and ministers obtained their mandates and positions through simple succession.

Bridges – **1** The longest bridge in the country connects Honshu with Shikoku. **2** A wooden bridge in Kyushu. **3** A stone bridge in Nagano. **4** Nihonbashi, the most famous bridge, has meanwhile been bridged over by Tokyo's highway. **5** Rainbow Bridge in Tokyo Bay. **6** Japan's oldest bridge in the Iiya Valley, on the island of Shikoku.

The Small, Creative Chaos
or a bit of anarchy in everyday life

Please excuse me if I have so far kept quiet about this: Japan is not a particularly neat and tidy country beyond its perfectly sorted pharmacies and book shops, its lovely gardens and uplifting shrines. And although its natural environment is stunning, many regions and the routes which you will probably tend to travel along as visitors to Japan (the main train lines and roads) are not particularly beautiful. You might find that large parts of the countryside, particularly in the immediate surroundings of the houses, look like badly run spare-parts stores or collection points for bulky waste. And the inhabitants don't seem to notice it. You could also quote the tough verdict of a few respected and widely traveled Japan observers who claim, without hesitation, that this is the ugliest country in the world. But I think that's a little too extreme.

Without doubt, Japan has an excess of products and a lack of storage places to put these things, if they aren't quite busted yet, but are simply no longer used. We must always remember that this island inherently hasn't got much space. As a consequence its people are blessed with the astounding ability of selective perception. Thus equipped they manage to turn a blind eye to certain objects which undeniably stand around uselessly and which objectively look awful. They either simply don't see them or else they are just not bothered by them.

In a country where there is no more storage space in the house and the garage is just large enough for one car, if you climb out via its trunk, in a country where there are no cellars or attics due to lack of space, earthquakes and the frequent murderous rains, there is a great temptation to store disused things elsewhere. Primarily in the area around the house. This is why crates, boxes, buckets and plastic bins, car wrecks, broken furniture and bicycles are disposed of temporarily in front of the door. Maybe there is this hope that this stuff will somehow disappear on its own. But it rarely does, so these things continue to stand around and aren't noticed by anyone due to their selective perception. And eventually the person who put the stuff there in the first place is oblivious to it, too. Interestingly, bicycles haunt certain strategic places like the plague. Preferred areas include any space under pedestrian bridges near train stations. They are parked there in huge numbers and become

1 A pair of trainers plus a tank of goldfish decorate this cabbage field. 2 Chaos on the beach of Aomori. 3 Bicycles really haunt every station area like the plague. 4 Why tidy up, if this works, too?

1 Crates, boxes and canisters pile up in front of the houses. 2 Often there'll be a bike standing around as well. 3 You'll see a tangle of cables in some streets.

an incredible tangle of wire, handle bars and tires during the day. This tangle is a nuisance as it reduces the walkway, which is narrow as it is, even further. Shopping sometimes becomes the purest bike handle slalom. But it is miraculous: nobody — except stressed foreigners, prone to high blood pressure, like myself — seems to notice it or be bothered about it in the slightest. Even though many of the rusty bikes which are carelessly leant against buildings or lanterns have flat tires, quite possibly since the Olympics in Tokyo.

And even if a truck from the city council does come by once in a while and the most obtrusive bikes are loaded with many apologies and carted off, it doesn't help much. The occasional loss of a bike is considered normal by most. It is part of the fight for survival for

anyone coming home late after a few drinks to borrow one of the bikes, which hasn't been locked up or carted off, to wheel home with it. Of course it is quickly forgotten, so it might soon become a permanent feature of and eyesore in the borrower's front yard, as many examples up and down the country prove. Apart from the bikes, there are other legal things that stand around at every street corner: vending machines for drinks. They are lit up brightly at night, contribute to the overall vista and are simply everywhere. But what there isn't at every street corner are public garbage cans. So the person dying of thirst who knows this, of course, is encouraged to pour his iced coffee, green ice tea, caffeine-containing soft drink or his peach-carrot juice down his throat there and then, as the only disposal option is the can bin right next to the dispenser. Yet sometimes it is full or else it has been stolen. In that case the empty cans are simply left next to the vending machines in silent protest.

The magical way things come together

The partially overwhelming chaos of seemingly eternally temporary solutions also has an extremely creative and artistic side to it. Suddenly objects which are actually unrelated in their form and content come together and express fundamental human desires and subtle messages in their intellectually stimulating composition. In Japan, spontaneous and sometimes permanent installations develop. Both in the cities and in rural areas. They develop on the side, by the way, unexpect-

edly and remain unnoticed by many. In many modern museums from New York to Berlin large crowds of people would form around such magical collections of things. An intense and heated discussion on the intentions and messages of the artist and the deep meaning of the work of art would be held.

Pars pro toto, I'll mention just a few installations with fish. The anonymous works of art are (probably) called: "A couple of goldfish in plastic bags in front of someone's door" (see p.35), "Two rubber boots and a rack of dried fish" (above) and "a pair of trainers plus three goldfish in a field of cabbages" (see p.154,1).

The small, everyday chaos is not only found on the surface of the earth, but has extended to airspace as well. In Japan, telephone and electricity cables are laid above ground. Nobody outside of this country understands why. Apparently it's supposed to be safer during earthquakes which, as we know, are quite frequent here. Of course the ignorant foreigner might remark that it doesn't seem very safe to be crushed by concrete pylons carrying heavy transformers and humming cables during an earthquake. But this remark doesn't sway the town planners and bureaucrats off course. They tell you in a slightly annoyed manner that the Japanese soils are simply different from the soils abroad. And I suspect that some generous mogul, who produces electricity pylons, is kept in a good mood. It certainly isn't the first and only infrastructure measure which has been based on similar considerations. Consequently some streets look as though invisible giant spiders have spun their

webs along them. Clumps of cables surround the transformers and the electricity connections swing to the next customer from relays which have been crudely stuck together. I feel sorry for the producers of the Samurai dramas which are so popular with the TV audience. Even in the least affected streets you have cables criss-crossing the scenery, consequently most of these dramas have to be filmed indoors. You can think what you may about the film The Last Samurai and its portrayal of Japanese culture and history. But the fact that not a single meter of it was filmed in Japan, that all of it was filmed in New Zealand, tells you a lot about the optical condition of this country. When the small town of Obanzawa in the prefecture of Yamaguta reacted to the complaints of frustrated hobby photographers and decided to lay the cables underground at last to free up the view of the old houses, this sensation was reported in the media throughout the entire country.

Japan's patterns – **1** Stop, not everything here is chaos. On the contrary – Japan is also a country of beautiful patterns. In small and large ways they enrich the aesthetics of every day life. **1** Wooden sandals. **2** Daruma, the Japanese wish dolls. **3** Ema, the wooden plaques at the shrines. **4** Kimonos. **5** Sponsor lanterns at the temple. **6** Funny inflatable toy animals. **7** Sad Buddha statues for the souls of aborted children.

The Magic of the Fire Flowers
Japan's midsummer night's dream

We have already established that nothing touches the Japanese as deeply as the transient magnificence of cherry blossoms and fall foliage and the – praise the Lord – transient sawing of the *semi*. The largest summer pleasure of the Japanese should be added to this list, too: the *hanabi*, the flowers made of fire.

Nobody knows exactly who brought fireworks to the island. Is this something else that the Chinese brought in, or was it the Portuguese? Whoever it was found a very grateful audience. As early as medieval times the Shoguns ordered fireworks to entertain the masses – and also to drive away the spirits of the dead. Nowadays there are at least 5000 fireworks displays per year in Japan. The biggest ones last an hour. During such a large display anywhere between 10,000 and 20,000 individual fireworks are shot off.

The balls are shot out from steel pipes. In the past each firework had to be lit with a cigarette. Nowadays this is done centrally with just the click of a mouse. The individual batteries are connected to the tent of the fireworks displayers by kilometers of cables.

Tokyo has two large *hanabi* festivals which are held near the Sumidagawa and Edogawa rivers in the east of the city. They are held at the end of July/beginning of August and attract more than a million spectators each year. Weeks before the actual event, individuals, student clubs and companies stake out their claim. Then, in the days running up to the festival, one of them guards their particular spot to ensure that nobody occupies it. They stay on the festival grounds day and night, in the boiling heat and the pouring rain, to defend their plastic tarpaulins against enemies. Even in the country of harmony and respect, some people lose all inhibitions if they want a good spot for the *hanabi*.

On the day of the Edogawa festival the wide banks of the river start to fill up with crowds of people from lunchtime onwards. This particular *hanabi* is the largest fireworks display in the world, measured by the number of spectators it attracts. Some are dressed in the colorful *yukatas*, the light summer kimonos, and look as though they've hopped straight out of a Japanese woodblock print of ancient times. Everyone is armed with a cooler full

1 A proper Japanese fireworks display goes on for at least an hour. **2** Each individual explosion is watched closely and enjoyed. **3** Between 10,000 and 20,000 individual fireworks are set off. **4** The fire flowers are perfectly round and look the same from every angle.

1 Days before the event, fans have staked their claims. 2 The fireworks organizers of Kagiya setting up their control center. 3 The fireballs are set off with the click of a mouse. 4 But every single one of them has to be put into its shot pipe first.

of beer and snacks. Come early evening there is not a single square centimeter in a three-kilometer stretch of meadow along the river which hasn't been occupied by someone. It is the largest picnic in the world. An annual Woodstock. The atmosphere is cheerful and peaceful. Even people who don't usually feel comfortable in large crowds will experience even the largest Japanese mass of people as pleasant and civilized.

And they are thrilled when the show finally starts, marked by a breathtaking explosion. Japanese fireworks fans do not "ooh" and "aah" quietly. Amano Akiki, the manager and chief designer of Kagiya, one of the largest and most traditional *hanabi* houses, observed that "the people in the West enjoy the whole atmosphere of a firework. But here in Japan it is different. The people here are very spoilt and also very knowledgeable. They judge every single explosion."

And yes, they scream with delight and acclaim every single successful image of flowers, chrysanthemums and peonies, which

Handmade fireballs

Japan's tradition-conscious pyrotechnicians don't work with rockets or firecrackers, but with round shells or balls which are all made by hand. Their mixture of gunpowder and a number of chemical additives is so explosive that mere friction could make them explode. They have to be handled very

carefully. Only balls can create these perfect images of fire. Why? Because they are perfectly round and the same image is created from any side. The smaller ones are approximately the size of a coconut, the larger ones weigh a ton and may not be set off in cities any longer for security reasons. They create an image about 350 meters across and are wrapped up in fourteen layers of paper so that they give off a huge bang when they explode.

opens up above them. It is a symphony of fire, underlined by music. Ms. Amano spends months composing, designing and improving all this. The colors and shapes, the rhythm and dramaturgy. They are majestic compositions of light and color, linking up with each other, engulfing each other. Another big bang, then a rain of fire in the shape of Mount Fuji with green spots above. Stars and faces and butterflies appear and then the night sky rains glowing rocket ash down onto the crowd. This doesn't frighten the people, it thrills them, as they can not only watch the fireworks display, they can also feel it.

And at the end, after non-stop fireworks for 75 minutes, the grand finale: a bombastic eruption of pink cherry blossoms.

You will hardly be able to find more devotion and enchantment than in the eyes of the spectators when the last star has died and the applause for this magic show starts slowly, engulfing the river banks like a wave.

Ms. Amano tells me, "This is the most beautiful moment for us. When we hear the applause and know that we have really given people dreams with our work."

Transient dreams, of course. But then, nothing touches the Japanese deeper than transience.

The Path of the Gods
Religion between tranquility and intoxication

Thanks to their religion, the Japanese have the most splendid historical buildings, some of the most interesting modern buildings, the greatest works of art and the longest traditions. But one may add that they aren't a particularly religious people, at least not in our sense of the word.

Their own religion is Shinto, the path of the gods. Shinto is a religion of nature. Every tree, every bush, certain rocks, a stream or a whole mountain, such as Mount Fuji, are not only inhabited by gods, but they are gods in themselves. There are over eight million gods which are devotedly referred to as *kami* or *kami-sama*. There are no holy scripts, no church services and no commandments in the Shinto religion. In principle, everybody can do whatever he or she wants. But it is a good idea to ask the gods for assistance occasionally. Particularly prior to a great new endeavor. Even in modern-day Japan no high-rise building is constructed and no fireworks display is started without Shinto priests setting up an altar of sacrifices with fruit, vegetables and fish and blessing the place and the main actors with their sticks to which white paper strips are attached. The Shinto religion also does not demand that people of other beliefs have to be converted. Shinto has established itself in Japan as a religion focused on the here and now, supporting the earthly quest for happiness and success.

Buddhism arrived in Japan in the year 552 (or maybe 538, it is hard to establish when exactly). It came, as so many other things, from China via Korea. Its most powerful supporter was Prince Shotoku, who is adored to this day. The worry that the local gods would not get on with this new religion proved unnecessary. Buddhism and Shinto get on just great and complement each other.

Buddhism serves as an anchor particularly for those who have to deal with questions of the afterlife, due to sickness or death within the family. The Japanese grieving ceremonies, funerals and burials are Buddhist. You will find most of the Buddha statues, which are often caringly supplied with crocheted caps and bibs, in cemeteries. The Japanese believe that they console the souls of dead children who haven't been able to enter paradise, as they saddened their parents so by dying.

But aside from the established religions, there are a considerable

1 The prayer hall in the Chion temple in Kyoto by night. **2** Fearsome lanterns at the nebuta- matsuri, Aomori. **3** Silent prayer at the large shrine of Izumo. **4** A turbulent festival – the torigoe-matsuri in the east of Tokyo.

1 The sea bream *matsuri* in Toyohama, near Nagoya. 2 The *onbashira-matsuri* in Suwa, the dangerous ride on the tree trunk. 3 The *kunchi* – the great *matsuri* of Nagasaki. 4 Healing smoke of the sacrifice fire at the Asakusa Kannon in Tokyo. 5 The great Buddha in Kamakura.

number of "new religions" and Buddhist sects which have millions of followers.

Christianity, which was brought to Japan by Francis Xavier in 1549, never achieved great importance. One of the reasons was that when it showed initial missionary successes it was gruesomely persecuted and almost eradicated by the jealous military leaders. Only in the region of Nagasaki did a few Christian communities survive the persecutions.

Nobody will be able to understand this country and its people without participating at least once at a *matsuri*, a shrine festival at which the local kami is celebrated.

The *kami* generally don't want much. Only once a year, during the matsuri, the *kami* want to be entertained. With a big ceremony they enter the *mikoshi*, the portable shrine which is opulently decorated with gold, and let themselves be carried and shoved through the neighborhood. The wilder the *mikoshi* is spun around

by its porters, the larger is the blessing that the *kami* gives to the community. There are hundreds, maybe thousands of different *matsuris* in this country. Every village, every municipality has a different date, a different deity and its own traditions and customs, which are centuries old, to honor its kami. But all the *matsuris* have one thing in common: during the feast it is not blood that flows in the veins of the Japanese – it is a cocktail of sake, adrenaline and testosterone. Once a year all inhibitions are dropped and all class differences are ignored. Peace-loving old-age pensioners turn into proud generals who order around the young people in their district. Obedient clerks mutate to charismatic party leaders, as soon as they don their traditional *matsuri* costumes. They whip up and steer the crowds, which vibrate full of joie de vivre. Well-behaved ticket conductors turn into jeering hooligans and studious students become lurching shrine bearers. Nothing that we thought we knew about Japan and its people holds true any longer. At a matsuri, the Japanese become cocky, frivolous, crazy.

You will most likely hear that a particular matsuri is "one of the three" largest, most significant or most beautiful feasts in Japan. Let's have a look at five beautiful *matsuris*. Each one of them could be nominated as "one of the three". What they all have in common is that they go on for three days (sometimes longer), during which life revolves around nothing else.

1. The most opulent costumes are displayed at the *kunchi*, the great festival of Nagasaki (beginning of October). This festival was initiated in the 17th century by the local military rulers to spoil the appetite of the Japanese for Christianity. Those in power felt that Christianity presented a threat, and as the Christian holidays and feasts attracted more and more followers, they set up something unmistakably Japanese as a counterforce. In the arena surrounding the Suwa shrine, rough guys whip the model ships, which are manned with children playing music, around and suddenly start running, only to come to a stop just before a very steep staircase. Strong men blindly balance round canopies made of splendidly embroidered fabrics, weighing hundreds of kilograms. And the descendants of the large Chinese community of this city balance monsters of papier-mâché, 15 meters long, through the crowd.

2. You'll come across the wildest crowds during the summer festivals in the east of Tokyo. They are the *kanda-, sanja- or torigoe-matsuris* (mid-May, end of May, beginning of July, respectively). Since hundreds

of years these wild processions have served to plead the gods for protection against diseases in the rainy season and the oppressive summer heat which is about to commence. The youths of each district assemble around their *mikoshi* and rock it, push it, shove it and battle with it through the narrow streets of Tokyo's old city. The highlight of the torigoe festival on the first Sunday in June consists of the *mikoshi* of the *torigoe* shrine, which is said to way a ton or more, being heaved from street to street by the local people. The inhabitants of each street take turns. When the *mikoshi* guides give the sign to move with their wooden instruments, the crowd starts to cheer and the golden heraldic bird on the roof of the portable shrine starts to tremble while the lurching, panting, stamping unearthly creature with a thousand hands and feet finds its way through the municipality. A sweating knot of human bodies breathing sake fumes, faces distorted with physical effort and rapture. In every house, every garage along the kilometer-long path of the procession there are parties and picnics.

3. The biggest lanterns of the country are displayed at the *nebuta-matsuri* in Aomori at the beginning of August. Here monsters at least 20 meters high and several meters wide are pulled along by dozens of bearers. They are Samurais, *kabuki* heroes and deities made of papier-mâché. Like so many of the summer festivals, the *nebuta* festival serves to drive away the exhaustion of summer and to prepare for the, hopefully, bountiful rice harvest. Troupes of drummers and flute players and thousands of elated people wearing strange colorful hats shouting "*Rasse-rah, rasse-rah*" dance between the huge floats and parade through the night-time streets of Aomori.

4. Each year in mid-July the fishermen and women of the small harbor community Toyohama, south of Nagoya, in the prefecture of Aichi, carry the most spectacular fish, a huge sea bream, through their village. The fishermen spend weeks making this monster, twenty meters long and weighing tons, out of bamboo and papier-mâché. First it is pulled into the harbor to remind the sea gods to

1 The Todaiji Temple in Nara, the largest wooden construction in the world, is home to a second sitting giant Buddha. 2 The bride is dressed in white – the end of a Shinto wedding. 3 A Shinto priest. 4 A Buddhist abbot.

continue to fill their fishing nets. Then the bream takes a trip through the village. During this procession the fisher people loudly sing old songs, some romantic and some of ruder content, and stop every hundred meters or so for a break and to keep up their mood with beer and sake. In the evening, for reasons unknown, the red brass is painted black and the following day it is rammed into a specially constructed toori and destroyed. The whole thing is accompanied by loud cheering.

5. Every six years, luckily not once a year, the men of Suwa, Nagano prefecture, experience the most dangerous downhill ride. They ride down a murderous slope on a tree trunk twenty meters long. The preparations for this feast start early. Long before the actual event, sixteen of the tallest fir trees are chosen high up in the mountains and are marked for felling. Their destiny is to be erected at the shrine of Suwa. As the festival draws nearer, the felled tree trunks are dragged down towards the valley, one at a time. They are dragged to the top of said murderous slope, where they are let go to slide down into the valley with several courageous men astride. More than one million spectators watch this event and broken bones and worse can be expected in the course of this death ride.

Undigested history

This of us who read the papers have heard about the Yasukuni Shrine in Tokyo. The Shrine always hits the main news when China or Korea object bitterly to the fact that a Japanese Prime Minister has visited it again to honor the souls of all Japanese soldiers that died in the various wars since 1853. The ghosts of the dead also turn into kami and they need the

attention and occasional homage of the living. These ghosts of the Yasukuni Shrine also include those of soldiers who were involved in the repression and colonization of Korea in 1910 and of soldiers who fought in World War II. And it also includes the souls of those who were executed as criminals of war when Japan collapsed. The shrine is a particularly important place for those families who lost their sons, brothers, fathers and husbands on faraway battlefields. There are no graves or bones over which they could grieve, so this is where they come to honor and remember their dead.

For Japan's neighbors and former victims, though, the Yasukuni Shrine is another example for the fact that the Japanese bluntly refuse to take any responsibility for the war and the atrocities they committed. This is a fact. The list of Japanese politicians who simply deny the crimes and massacres that the emperor's army committed is long. And still they keep their jobs. Japan's school books avoid this period of history in the most embarrassing way. They dedicate two only two lines to the bloody years of war in China and many other battle places in Asia, but devote more than two pages to the atom bombs. So Japan's government officials regularly ignore the loud protest from Seoul and Beijing and continue to go on a pilgrimage to the Yasukuni Shrine, as though nothing had happened. Probably to appease their many conservative voters and to prove that Japan has nothing to be ashamed of, nothing for which it needs to apologize.

Toori – means gate. A *toori* marks the entrance to a Shinto shrine. Next to the Fuji, they are probably the best-known Japanese symbols. They come in four varieties and three construction materials: wood, stone or iron. **1** Possibly the most famous of them all: the *toori* of Miyajima. **2** You'll often see shrines in the modern residential parts of towns. **3** At the hot springs of Beppu. **4** Every stone, tree or stream can be a *kami,* according to the Shinto belief. **5** Mighty: the *toori* at the entrance to the Meiji Shrine. **6** A small village shrine in Nagano.

The Dance with the Lanterns...

... and burning candles

The beginning of August, every year, is the time of the *kanto-matsuri* in Akita. You guessed it: it is one of the three largest matsuri in northern Japan. The word *kanto* describes a lantern tree around twelve to sixteen meters high, weighing 50–60 kilograms and bearing 24–46 paper lanterns with burning candles (!).

There are a few theories and explanations for the strange urge of the people of Akita to carry countless numbers of these lantern trees with the burning candles through their city at this time of the year. Some sources suggest that this custom started as a kind of ritual of catharsis: the people wanted to relieve themselves, through a civilized street parade, of the exhaustion of the hot summer and the sins which accumulated during this season. Initially they tried doing this by using leafy branches – with limited success. But when candles arrived in Japan in the 15th century, people thought they were perfect for the job. Especially as such festive, ceremonial events were also always used to beg the gods to spare them from diseases and disasters. Also, since August has always been the month, since ancient times, to call the souls of the dead (*o-bon*). Candles are best suited for this purpose, too. And like every matsuri, this event, too, contains the plea for a good harvest. Honestly speaking, I don't fully understand all this either, but I have learnt not to ask too many questions in Japan, particularly with regard to the matsuri, as it easily makes people feel embarrassed. That's simply the way it is, and that's the way it is done. Just so. Our grandfathers and fathers have done it this way, and it is great fun, and the kids enjoy it, too. Therefore that's the way we do it. This explanation, conversely, is one I am happy with, especially since it is totally sufficient for the people concerned.

At the *matsuri* the people of each district appear in their own distinctive costumes (*happi*). The aim of carrying around the lantern trees and performing tricks with them is to earn fame and honor for their particular part of town. The feast begins just like any *matsuri*. It starts in the early morning at the shrine where the Shinto priest blesses the participants with his ceremonial stick adorned with white paper strips, asking the gods that this time, too, nobody is seriously harmed or loses his eyesight, his physical health or his life.

1 Some lantern trees seem to have legs. **2** Balancing act – the lantern trees dance on hips, shoulders and foreheads. **3** Final check: does the headband look O.K.? **4** Each district has its own lantern tree.

The lantern heroes spend the rest of the day packing up their lanterns, drinking lots of beer and eating lots of fried delicacies. This matsuri is a feast for the young and the old, just like all the others, and it is always touching to see how everybody really bothers about the kids. Everybody knows that they are the future of these festivals and that they especially should enjoy the matsuri and eventually carry on the tradition. It works – even the coolest youths with dyed hair and nose piercings really get into it. Family members who have emigrated to faraway cities come back home for the matsuri and get swept up in all the excitement, as though they had never left.

In the late afternoon the lantern bearers start moving towards the town center where the spectacle is due to begin shortly after sun-

set. Several hundred thousand spectators from all around the country line the main street to watch the long procession of the individual districts with their kanto. The procession is accompanied by the typical flute and drum music, churning up the crowds. And then they are erected – 100 lantern trees grow simultaneously, right up into the dark sky of the night, cheered on by the crowd. Personally that would have been enough of a spectacle for me. But it continues. Now the young men, full of high spirits, hop, jump and dance through the streets with their huge lantern trees. They add another piece and another and let the trees grow higher and higher until the entire construction starts to bend to form a perilous arch with all the paper lanterns and the burning candles! They present each other with their kanto. And everybody gets the opportunity to prove his skill and courage.

That in itself would be alarming enough, but only now does the real fun begin: the lantern bearers start to balance their heavy load playfully on their hips, their shoulders and sometimes even on their

1 Hundreds of lantern trees are carried along the main street in the evening. **2** The matsuri starts with the blessing of the Shinto priest. **3** When the trees tip over, the crowds clap and cheer. **4** A feast for both young and old.

Bamboo for all circumstances

The preparations for the *kanto-matsuri* start years before the actual event. Each commune chooses its bamboo poles and prepares them. The only type of bamboo suitable for the kanto-matsuri is the madake *(Phyllostachys bambusoides)*. It has to be three years old and have segments around 22 centimeters apart. Of 300 bamboo trunks there'll only be one which can be used as a *kanto* pole.

In Japan you find 400–500 of the 1000 species of bamboo known worldwide. Some of these species grow naturally,

some are cultivated. Since ancient times the Japanese have used bamboo to make things for daily use and for decorative purposes. Apart from lantern masts, the *madake* is also suited for making the Japanese flute, the famous *shakuhachi*. The bamboo lends this instrument its unique, melancholy sound. The smaller species of bamboo are used to make walking sticks or fishing rods and, of course, the notorious washing poles. But baskets, too, and umbrella frames and chopsticks, ikebana vases and certain accessories for the tea ceremony are made of bamboo.

Once the trunks for the lantern trees have been selected carefully, they have to be stored in a dry place (usually the garage of the head of the district) for two to three years and then they have to be hardened over a fire. But the district and community associations of Akita, whose whole pride are their lantern trees, know all this.

foreheads. Then the representatives of the rivaling districts start dancing around each other, so of course sooner or later one or more kanto collide and tip over.

Instead of fearing for their lives (like myself), the crowd cheers, claps and shouts, full of joy, although it is only separated from the tumbling avalanches of lanterns (and burning candles) by thin ropes.

I think at least I have understood one thing about Japan: It needs and enjoys these small and large outbursts of overwhelming joie de vivre, of danger, intoxication and thrill. They balance its people.

And if you have ever sat under the swaying lanterns in Akita, you will know how important balance is…

Zen and the Quest for Freedom
A visit to Eiheiji monastery

The temple of eternal peace – Eiheiji. Could there be a more beautiful name? Eiheiji is a Buddhist monastery. It was founded over 750 years ago and is a small town in itself, consisting of a total of 70 buildings. It is located in the mountains of the Fukui prefecture, framed by steep slopes covered with cedars. It is a place for meditation. Eiheiji is Japan's most famous Zen monastery, the center of the *Soto* school of those Zen followers who seek enlightenment in the sitting meditation (*zazen*). The other school, the Rinzai sect, believes in the enlightening effect of unsolvable riddles.

At the onset of the so-called Kamakura period (1185–1333), when the first shoguns established their rule in the seaside town south of Tokyo, Zen was the guiding philosophy of the warrior class whose ideals matched well with the strictly ritualized, ascetic, no-frills virtue. Zen deeply influenced the Japanese sense of aesthetics, from the design of gardens, to calligraphy, to the tea ceremony. And for many people in Europe and America who are tired of our so-called "civilization", Zen seems to represent the promise to finally find sense and meaning in a world which is becoming more and more hectic and complex. At Eiheiji foreigners are welcomed as students of Zen. They usually only join short seminaries, as there are not many Westerners who are so intent on finding a meaning to their lives that they would be willing to submit themselves to the strict rules of the monastery for months or even years on end. The schooling of the Zen monks, which is run in accordance with ancient rules, aims at the detachment of the students from the five human wishes: possession, sex, food, esteem and sleep.

Whoever wants to leave these things behind will try to be admitted to Eiheiji. That in itself

requires a lot of determination and the ability to suffer, as the newcomers are left to wait in the cold, thinly clad, sometimes for hours. They are rejected again and again and criticized. This is how their motives and their aptitude is tested. Whoever is not deemed worthy has to leave.

But whoever passes this first test will spend the next days and weeks in the lotus position, doing zazen, sitting meditation. The

1 Breakfast in the monastery – rice pap with pickled vegetables. **2** In winter the airy corridors of the monastery are horribly cold. **3** Still the monks are barefooted... **4** ... during the big cleaning spree every morning.

1 The floor has to shine and sparkle. 2 Zazen – if one of the students shows signs of fatigue, he receives a blow with the stick. 3 Their cutlery and their clothes are the only personal belongings of the monks. 4 Windows and walls are polished, too. 5 Morning prayer in the large prayer hall.

novices sit in front of a wall from early morning to evening and try not to think about anything. Later on there are only two zazen sittings – one in the morning after the wake-up call (3.30 am in the summer and 4.30 am in the winter) and a second one in the evening. In winter the sitting is held in a cool ten degrees centigrade or so.

A monk walks up and down behind the row of those meditating, holding a stick. The stick is used to give those students showing signs of fatigue a loud – and probably quite painful – blow on the shoulder. With the path of complete mental emptiness and concentrating on nothing, the spirit is to be relieved of all earthly questions, worries and distractions to eventually find enlightenment.

The prayer hours, during which the old Buddhist Sanskrit texts are recited, serve the same aim. A monotonous, solemn chorus lulls the mind in a comforting fog of foreign words and sounds.

These prayers are chanted for the benefit of humanity as a whole and particularly for the benefit of those who have given donations and other forms of financial support to the monastery. It is a Buddhist peculiarity that you can, to a certain extent, buy yourself free of the duty to pray yourself by paying monks to do it for you. It is neither cynical, nor unreligious, it is simply customary and encouraged by the monks who need food and clothes and need to maintain their monastery. In Eiheiji they openly admit that they could hardly exist if their monastery weren't one of the large tourist attractions of Fukui with more than a million paying visitors per year (who don't experience a lot of the real monastery life of course, but are merely allowed to walk along its spacious corridors).

Breakfast is only served after zazen and the morning prayers. Of course all meals are vegetarian. Rice and pickled vegetables, without any spices – merely a little salt and sesame seeds are allowed. For lunch *miso* (soybean paste) soup and fried tofu is served. On days which end with a 4 or a 9, small potatoes are dished out, too. Apart from that, the monks are allowed a bath and a head shave on these days. Carrots, garlic and leek cause impure wishes to arise and are thus kept off the menu. Each monk spreads out his bundle containing his cutlery in front of him and eats his meal slowly and solemnly. His bundle of cutlery is his only personal belonging apart from his clothes.

As soon as they have finished eating, the monks, of which there are incidentally around 200, become active for about an hour, in contrast to their usual calm, meditative ways. Every one of them receives a rag and a big cleaning spree commences. Not a single bit of fluff and not a single grain of dust is allowed to remain. Windows, beams, the icy cold wooden floor which they run across with bare feet, everything is wiped and polished until it shines. Cleaning is a spiritual exercise, too. In the process the monks purify themselves, their thoughts, their minds. A day without work is a day without a meal. This is a traditional saying, not only a Buddhist saying. Finally the day at the monastery ends at 9 p.m. The monks lie down on their right sides, facing Buddha.

Thus they search the condition of enlightenment, the *satori*: the absence of all wishes, desires and crises, of all vanities and all questions. They search and some of them find it: enlightenment, complete freedom. Is this yet another one of the many paradoxes and riddles of this enigmatic country? Some of them find freedom in a life which consists of nothing but strict rules and bans, irrevocable laws and curricula centuries old.

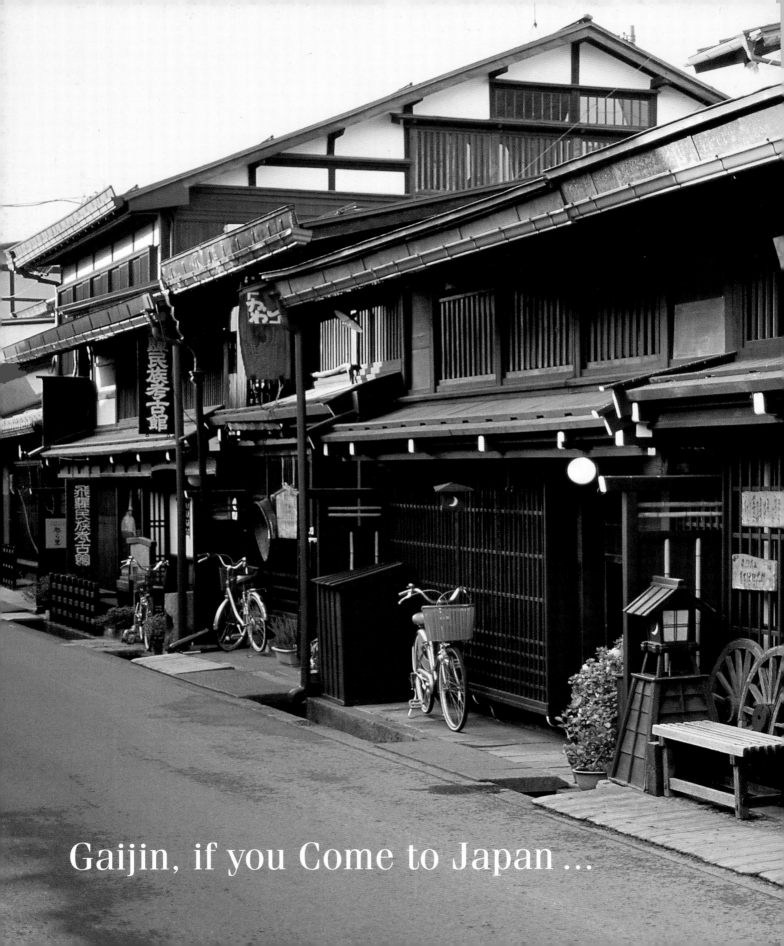

Gaijin, if you Come to Japan ...

A Few Instructions for the Visitor to Japan

The lovely thing about Japan is that we foreigners (gaijin) actually enjoy complete freedom to do whatever we want as soon as we have passed passport control and customs. The reason being that the majority of the Japanese secretly consider us incorrigible brutes (or better said: idiots without any manners). Why? On the one hand, because some of us really behave like that. On the other hand, even those Japanese who have good intentions simply don't know any better. But that's not so bad. Having learnt the hard way, the Japanese are quicker than others to forgive behavior which does not adhere to their customs. But I have to emphasize that they do not forgive rude and tactless behavior. Whoever loses face once by behaving abusively, crudely or arrogantly won't have a chance of being accepted. Ever!
Of course he won't be told that directly. But if you understand the signs, you'll understand…

Don't even try to learn how to bow correctly (except if you have reason to apologize vehemently for something). Even if you've learnt it (and it is very, very difficult and sometimes hurts) you'll often bow to the outstretched hand of the other person – and that's very embarrassing. Don't greet back gushingly if the girls in the pretty uniforms bow to you in the department store. Just behave as though you expected no different, as though this way of being greeted is completely normal for you and not something unexpected. In fact it actually is completely normal and doesn't express anything else but the happy expectation that you will be spending your money there.

Don't feel sorry for old people in uniforms who bow to you if a construction site is in your way. These people are merely doing their job and are proud of it. If you want to do them a favor, just don't fall into the construction pit.

Leave your laced boots at home, they'll be a nuisance in Japan where you are required to permanently take off your shoes. (It may be worthwhile considering the introduction of this pleasant and hygienic custom at home, too). Check that your socks don't have holes and consider using foot deodorant.

Bring gifts! Many! For everybody! Never visit someone

On the other hand the Japanese have great sympathy for the type of mistakes we are all known to make occasionally. But active forgiveness requires an active apology. The feeling of shame is possibly the strongest emotion in this country, and no Japanese will reject an honest apology, if it is delivered with an appropriate amount of sorrow and remorse as well as a bow in a right angle. Then the extent of their readiness for forgiveness is larger than anywhere else I've been. Countless court cases, arrests, fistfights and numerous murders simply don't take place, because somebody apologized properly before things got out of hand.

In general you will fare well and according to the rules if you avoid being brash. So don't entertain a whole subway carriage with your conversation. Apart from the loudspeaker announcements it is always quiet on the trains. Don't put your arm around someone's shoulder patronizingly, especially if you've never set eyes on that person before. Don't stand around with your friends as though you owned the world. And please, if you're traveling as a couple, never kiss in public!

without bringing a gift. But don't bring flowers or pieces of china, it is best to stick to something to nibble at. A small snack is sufficient to demonstrate that you are a nice, caring person! Don't embark on any trip in this country without buying a local delicacy (okashi – nibbles or pickles) for your host family, your friends or your business partners.

Accept a business cards passed to you with both hands, lift it slightly and study it briefly as though it were a check for over 10,000 euros. If you are sitting around a table with several people, lay out the business cards in front of you in accordance with the seating arrangement. Hand out your business cards with both hands, too and say: "Yoróshku onegáishimas!"

1 As a gaijin you will always stick out of a crowd – whether you wear a red wooly hat or not. 2 It is touching the way the Japanese try to welcome foreigners. 3 The golden rule is: remove your shoes whenever you visit someplace. 4 Tokyo is the city of the 10,000 taxis. 5 Confusing – the control panel of a modern Japanese toilet.

어서 오십시오

您可来了

Benvenuti

freudig begrüben

Soyez le bienvenue

Entren señores

welcome

Be careful at dinner: Japan's beer glasses are microscopically small. This is deliberate. The glasses have to be refilled permanently. And when your host refills your glass you should raise your glass slightly and thank him with a nod or a small grunt of approval. If his glass is empty, refill it for him! Don't ever refill your own glass!

Don't ever stick your chopsticks into the remaining rice after a meal! Not under any circumstances, even if you think it may look attractive!

Don't ever get impatient or even loud if something doesn't happen the way you want it to. Even if you feel you're right and even if in fact you are right. Even though it (whatever it is) works just so and no different at home. Even if you think that whatever is required from you is superfluous and ludicrous. Instead, take a deep breath and think of something lovely. Try to smile, even though it might make you look like a crocodile whose stomach ulcer is about to burst.

Don't call the waiter of a restaurant if you want to pay. The bill will be somewhere on or near your table without fail and you pay at the cashier's (if you've had a meal at a conveyor belt sushi, your plates will be counted).

Forget everything you've ever learnt about tips – they don't exist here. Not in the restaurant, not in the taxi, not in the hotel. The only exception that I know of are: geishas. They get a regal tip! Just get up from your table at the restaurant and say *"Gotschsoosama-deschta!"* You'll leave a good impression.

Say *"Doomo"* the whole time. This means "a lot" or "thank you" and will cast a favorable light on you.

What else?

The toilets!
If you've traveled through southern Europe, you won't feel too helpless about the Japanese crouch toilets. But you might feel helpless about the many dials and buttons and control panels of the modern Japanese seat toilets. Not even the NASA has produced anything like it. Careful: don't touch anything! Don't press any buttons if you cannot read what might happen if you do! Otherwise you'll suddenly be hit by a well-directed jet of warm water and in the worst case you won't know how to turn it off again. The crafty engineers of this country have invented an integrated bidet. It is a miracle why none of them have been awarded an international prize for it yet. The toilet seats are heated, too. This is a luxury which nobody will be able to appreciate until he or she has experienced it. Why do we buy Japanese cars and TVs, but not Japanese toilets?

The baths!
We talked about this before. Scrub, wash, rinse and shower yourself visibly and properly (without leaving traces of soap suds!) before you lower yourself into the public bath. Then – just to be on the safe side – scrub, wash and shower yourself again. Don't put on your bathing trunks or your bathing costume and don't even consider taking your dirty laundry with you to wash in the baths. (I am saying this only because it is a topic on the posters illustrating the dos and don'ts for foreigners, just to be on the safe side, which you will come across in most of the public baths.)

The nose!
Avoid blowing your nose loudly in public. On the other hand it is completely acceptable – and apparently also much more healthy – to snuffle. This also means that it is considered very impolite to give your neighbor in a plane or train, after he has been driving you crazy with his sniffing and snuffling for the past two hours, an angry look. And refrain from grimly offering him a tissue.

Taxis!
Don't wave around like mad if you want to stop a taxi. The drivers are attentive and will notice the smallest hand sign. With a brief flash of the warning lights they'll signal that they have seen you. The cab's rear door facing away from the street will open and close automatically. Although more and more taxis are equipped with navigation systems, keep a map ready of where you want to go, especially if it is a private address.

I honestly cannot think of anything else.
And you don't need to know anything else.
You'll get on just fine in Japan.
Don't be afraid!
Be curious and open!
Don't get nervous and impatient!
Smile!
Nod!
Say *"Doomo"*!
These things which seem so insignificant will open up a whole new world to you in this enigmatic country.

Well, Where Should We Go...?
Travel guide to Japan's top ten destinations

If at this point I were to wonder whether I should really recommend the long, tiring and maybe expensive trip to this enigmatic country to you, I'd come to the following conclusion after very careful consideration: yes, absolutely! Come to Japan! Come quick, regardless of everything. You won't find another place on our planet, except for the depths of the oceans, where so many things are so different from what we are used to. But still so pleasant, without friction, so colorful and harmonious. Come, although and especially because Japan is relatively unknown to this day and is unprepared for a surge of foreign visitors. This is precisely what makes this country so different to any other.

We often travel to countries which realized decades ago how important tourism can be economically. In Japan this realization is only just dawning on them. For a long time the Japanese economic strategists considered irrelevant anything which could not be produced on a conveyor belt and exported. A recent survey of the hotels in the prefecture of Shizuoka showed that 40 percent of the hotels would rather do without foreign visitors, as they did not feel confident that they could face the challenges that would come with them. The Japanese obviously consider themselves difficult and not presentable and they fear the complications which inevitably arise when they come into contact with foreigners. Consequently they prefer to stay amongst themselves. Do you see what I mean? Japan needs us! But do we need Japan? Sometimes we do. We need the wonderful experience of being a complete stranger, helpless in an ultra-modern country which copies the Western lifestyle on the surface. In a country which knows and enjoys the pizza, the microwave and all the other creature comforts of our world, but one in which we do not know the language and sit helplessly in the taxi (as the taxi driver usually needs accurate instructions, unless you want him to take you to the station, the airport or the Emperor's Palace) or wander around at night through parts of town where lights flash and all the foreign signs intimidate us. This experience matures us and

makes us better people. If you cannot decipher the menu and cannot even agree on the word "breakfast buffet" with the guy at reception, you'll realize that there actually still are precious islands which are different and unique in this mercilessly globalized world. And one of these islands is certainly Japan.

You might feel lost, but you won't feel left alone. People will look after you, offer to help you, accompany you to your hotel, if need be on foot even if it is ten blocks away, or by car if it turns out that the hotel you're looking for is in a different part of town. Many Japanese know all too well what it feels like to be stranded abroad without having a clue about the language or the place. And you'll rarely be left staring helplessly at a public city map of Tokyo for more than ten seconds, before hearing a friendly *"May I help you?"* (This is one of the few widespread English sentences. Whoever tells you that you won't have any problems getting through with English has either never been to Japan or has experienced a complete miracle.)

I don't want to prescribe where you should travel to. Everybody will be looking for something different, and inveterate Japan fans will not choose the same destinations as newcomers, who are often grateful when they have a chance just to wander through Tokyo, Kamakura and Nikko and at the most get to know Kyoto and Nara as well. This country has such a diversity that you won't be able to discover everything, even if you spend years traveling in it.

But I would like to recommend a few places to you. A few places which I have visited myself and which I will never forget. Others may prefer different places, but those are some of my favorite spots. And what you won't be able to see in my photos are the wonderful people that I met there and the delicious food I was spoilt with. The lovely air that I breathed and the occasional feeling that I had discovered something special. The following is a very personal list of my top ten destinations in Japan.

1. Mount Mitoku-san

Mount Mitoku-san in the prefecture of Tottori is at the very top of my list. It is a real insider's tip which is not mentioned much in any travel guide. The sight of the wooden temple Nageire-do, which is built into the rocks, is stunning! It has been used as a place for meditation for 800 years. You will never forget its beauty – and you certainly won't forget the ascent! Whoever came here in previous centuries sought peace and solitude. Even in a Japanese travel guide the description is merely. "After a good hour of quite a difficult climb, you will reach…" In this case "difficult" doesn't only imply that the path is steep. In parts you have to climb straight up the rock face, but without the help of steps or stones. You have to hang on to the roots of old trees. After a mountain tour of almost one and a half hours, without any guard rails, finally balancing across a rock the size of a house, next to which there is nothing but the yawning precipice, we – a German TV journalist, moderately sporty, plus his film editor and wife who suffers from vertigo – reached our destination. And en route we were overtaken again and again by cheerful Japanese old-age pensioners. But you forget these exertions when you stand up there in front of the

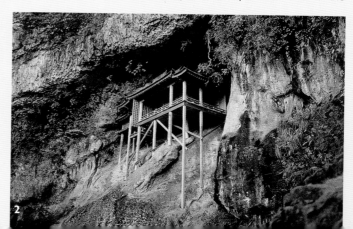

gray rock wall, staring up at the incredible construction of the Nageire-do above you, with the densely vegetated mountain slopes behind.

2. Shimanto-gawa River

One of the few rivers which the bureaucrats in Tokyo have not yet forced into a concrete corset or destroyed by dams is the second longest river of Shikoku in the southwestern part of the prefecture of Kochi. It is a clean, calm river, full of fish. It meanders through picturesque valleys, framed by a pebble bed which in places is twice as broad as the river itself. Small forgotten villages are dotted along its banks. Raptorial birds soar above, midges do their dance, only occasionally does a leisure boat cruise by. This is purest natural paradise according to Japanese standards.

3. The Izu Peninsula

In only two hours' drive you'll reach the most adventurous cliff coasts and the dreamiest sandy beaches in the region southwest of Tokyo. If you avoid Atami and keep driving south you'll reach the small town of Shimoda, which every Japanese has heard about. This is the place where in July 1853 the notorious "black ships" of US Commodore Perry landed to force the shogun to give up his policy of self-isolation and to open up the Japanese

1 Taxi drivers need detailed instructions. **2** The Nageire-do, a temple like an eagle's nest. **3** Japan's most beautiful coast – the rocky coast of Izu. **4** Shimanto-gawa River in Kyushu runs its natural course.

ports to US ships. Shimoda (and Hakodate in Hokkaido) became the first Japanese port in which foreigners secured landing rights and set up their own representation for themselves. Up to that point merely a few Dutch were allowed to dwell on an artificial island in the port of Nagasaki. South of Shimoda, a sleepy small town with hardly any signs of its historical significance, apart from a Perry memorial near the port and a small alley with old houses, the hiking trails follow the rocky coastline where the Pacific waves come thundering in. A word of caution: be prepared to come across snakes here. By the way, you'll get the best views of Mount Fuji from the west coast of the peninsula. These views are depicted on most of the sento walls.

4. Takachiho Canyon
According to the legends, the sun goddess Amaterasu Omikami hid in a cave here in the mountains of today's prefecture of Miyazaki on Kyushu. And while she had disappeared, night fell over the world. Maybe this is an indication of the origin of this dramatic canyon. It was formed 30,000 years ago after a mighty eruption of the Aso volcano. This place is deeply linked to the Japanese myths. It is a playing field for the gods and the spirits. The tight canyon, with its rock faces covered in moss, is five kilometers long. A wild mountain river rushes through it and a waterfall cascades into it at its bottom end (or its top end, depending on which direction you enter it from). Every evening farmers and amateur actors stage a god dance at the shrine up on the mountain. They wear masks (kagura) and their dance narrates the legend of the sun goddess. She hid away in the cave, disgusted by the wild goings-on of her brother Susanoo Mikoto. She only emerged again when the gods tricked her cleverly: they giggled and laughed in front of the cave, making her wonder what was so amusing. Obviously Japan's gods always liked fun and entertainment. They still do.

5. Kurashiki Port
The side of Honshu facing the Inland Sea between the urban agglomeration of Osaka/Kobe down to Hiroshima is mainly an ugly moon landscape with small patches of industrial develop-

ment, full of chimney stacks and oil storage tanks, which have developed wherever the steep hills and mountains rendered it possible. And if you drive through the town of Kurashiki in Okayama prefecture, you'll probably wonder whether it was as rotten idea to leave the highway. Today you wouldn't guess that, in the medieval times and during the Meiji period, this town with its 450,000 inhabitants was a significant center for trade. Mainly the textile trade. The textiles were stored here in warehouses along a canal before they were loaded onto ships heading for Osaka. Similar to Takayama, what remains of the old city is limited to two or three streets, but these few streets are definitely worth visiting, particularly for those interested in fine arts, as many of the old warehouses have been converted into modern museums.

6. The village of Shirakawago
This village is held in high esteem and has been idealized in countless photographs in travel catalogs and on posters in tourism offices. It is said to still have the highest density of farmhouses, which still give you a feel for the rural life which once defined these islands. Houses with steep roofs, thatched with reeds – yes, there are still many of them here. But I don't know if I should find it quirky or a shame that even here, at this internationally

renowned destination and World Heritage property, the ugly electricity pylons and cables destroy any illusion of historical authenticity. And that today you find the ubiquitous often very shabby yards, disfigured with corrugated iron and always full of rusty car wrecks, right between the lovely old farmhouses. Especially since, after all, real live farmers still live in many of the old houses and the village isn't purely a museum for folklore. Shirakawago isn't exactly easy to get to though. It is at least another 90-minute drive from Takayama. In winter it is almost impossible to get there because of the snow and ice. In summer it is abuzz with bussed-in tourists, which shows yet again: the Japanese yearn for sights and experiences of their own history. It is a crying shame that there are so few of them.

7. Takayama city

As I have said before, the Japanese do not treat their historical buildings with care. Old buildings are expensive to keep and to restore. And even if they have been restored, they are still frighteningly old and frequently uncomfortable to live in afterwards. Whatever is old is generally considered antiquated and outdated. Therefore there are only a few streets in Japan which have been preserved in their original form. (And when I say that I mean: ignore the road signs and the Coke vending machines.) The two streets of Takayama, which are listed, certainly belong to these few. But whoever assumes that the houses harbor anything but souvenir shops, restaurants and tourist-friendly sake breweries doesn't understand Japanese tourism. During peak season you'll hardly be able to squeeze through the crowds of tourists from all over Japan. And Japanese tourism is vibrant and loud. Come and have a look at it! But avoid the business hours!

8. The Meiji Mura Museum

Nagoya is a huge city which looks fantastic seen by night from the plane, but I found that it looks a little drab when I walked through it during daytime. But I have to admit that I have never spent any more time than necessary in Nagoya and I find that more or less all of Japan's cities appear drab. So it is all the more relaxing to take a trip to the nearby town of Inuyama where you'll find one of the most incredible open-air museums in the country, the meiji village (meiji-mura). If you want to find out about the Japanese history of modern times, about its mistakes and successes, you should spend at least one whole day in the over 60 buildings which have been reconstructed true to the originals on a large site of 100 hectares. Banks, bridges, factories, hotels, stores, hospitals, government buildings and a full-scale cathedral. Some of these buildings stood somewhere in the country up to the 1960's. They were then taken apart, stone for stone, plank for plank, and reassembled again here. It is a cemetery for missed opportunities for city development, but also a treat for visitors to Nagoya who are interested in history.

1 Takachiho Canyon. 2 Fall in the warehouse town of Kurashiki. 3 Lovingly restored buildings from all around the country can be admired in the meiji-mura.

9. The beach of Jodogahama

The Japanese don't really care much for beach life. This makes this beach on the Pacific coast of the Iwate prefecture even more special. It consists of pebbles, and you look out over strangely shaped white cliffs. The waves gently lick the shore and the water is dotted with swimmers and people looking for easily digestible delicacies along the cliffs and rocks. Several steep and challenging hiking trails start from this beach and lead you along the craggy coast to lonely beaches. But please note that "lonely beaches" are defined such in Japan: there's an angler at every available spot and on every rock. These people simply love angling more than anything else. Unfortunately I can't say any more about Jodogahama, as my attention was mainly absorbed by a young woman and her pet, a ferret. She held the ferret by a leash and couldn't understand why the stupid animal wasn't enjoying the day on the beach, but kept on wanting to dive into her bag. What the women didn't see was a majestic bird of prey which was drawing its circles meditatively above the nervous ferret. This is the type of extremely entertaining encounter you may have occasionally in this country full of variety.

10. Shikaribetsu Lake

This is a comparatively small, almost enchanted lake in Hokkaido, the wild northern island of Japan. And you are relatively safe from bears here. (I was very relieved to be told this, as I would never have forgiven myself to have to read the following words on my gravestone in the 21st century: Here lies Gert Anhalt. He was eaten by a bear.) As opposed to the large tourist centers of the island, this lake is not easily accessible. There is only one road, in pretty poor condition, which runs from the plain near the cities of Obihiro and Kushiro out through a mountain landscape which unfortunately I cannot say much about, as it was shrouded in fog while I was there. Here there are – or were – none of the usual luxury hotels with 1000 beds, and no fun baths with 14 pools, just three or four inns in a small bay exactly opposite Lip Mountain. Its name is derived from the fact that the reflection of its two tops in the water has the shape of a mouth.

1 The cliffs at Jodogahama beach make an idyllic backdrop for a little picnic and relaxation. 2 Romantic morning mood at Lip Mountain.

Index

At Yamadera tempel in Yamagata: *Hotei*, one of the seven goddesses of fortune, is responsible for **wealth and fertility**.

Imprint

Author and Photographer
Gert Anhalt (born in 1963 in Bad Wildungen, Germany) completed his degree in Japanese Studies in Marburg, Germany, and in Tokyo. From 1993 on he worked as a television correspondent for the ZDF, a public German TV channel, in Beijing and was transferred to Tokyo in 2000. He is also the author of a detective series. His pen name is Raymond A. Scofield. A passionate photographer since childhood, he took photos of motifs in Japan which words could not adequately describe.

Cover photos
Front large photo: the mikoshi of the Torigoe Matsuri; small photos: geisha (t.l.), rocks of Kamaishi (t.c.), sushi (t.r.)
Back Fuji-san, a photo artwork by the almost blind Makoo Aikawa

Page one sacrificial offering for the big Buddha of Kamakura

Photo credits:
Makoto Aikawa, Tokyo, pp. 28/29 and backcover
Christine Anhalt, Tokyo, p. 28 t.c.
Toby Marshall, Tokyo: pp 50/51, portrait of the author
all others: Gert Anhalt

This work has been carefully researched by the author and kept up to date as well as checked by the publisher for coherence. However, the publishing house can assume no liability for the accuracy of the data contained herein.

For the team of the ZDF-studios in Tokyo, used to facing danger and suffering: Christine, Tob, Fuyuko, Lilo and Ota-san.
And for Ikuta Koshin, who has never left us.

We are always grateful for suggestions and advice. Please send your comments to:
C.J. Bucher Publishing, Product Management
Innsbrucker Ring 15
81673 Munich
Germany
e-mail:
editorial@bucher-publishing.com
Homepage:
www.bucher-publishing.com

Translation: Jenny Baer, Mayerling, Austria
Proof-reading: Patricia Preston, Munich, Germany, and Asa Tomash, Maine, USA
Design: Werner Poll, Munich, Germany, revised by Agnes Meyer-Wilmes, Munich
Cartography: Astrid Fischer-Leitl, Munich, Germany

Product management for the German edition: Joachim Hellmuth
Product management for the English edition: Dr. Birgit Kneip
Production: Bettina Schippel
Repro: Repro Ludwig, Zell am See
Printed in Italy by Printer Trento

© 2007 C.J. Bucher Verlag GmbH, Munich

ISBN 978-3-7658-1624-6